Shut Your Eyes and Think of England

A Comedy

JOHN CHAPMAN and ANTHONY MARRIOTT

SAMUEL FRENCH

LONDON
NEW YORK SYDNEY TORONTO HOLLYWOOD

© 1978 by Anthony Marriott and John Chapman

This play is fully protected under the Copyright Laws of the British Commonwealth of Nations, the United States of America and all countries of the Berne and Universal Copyright Conventions.

All Rights, including Stage, Motion Picture, Radio, Television, Public Reading and Translation into Foreign Languages are strictly reserved.

No part of this publication may lawfully be transmitted, stored in a retrieval system, or reproduced in any form or by any means, electronic, mechanical, photocopying, manuscript, typescript, recording, or otherwise, without the prior permission of the copyright owners.

Rights of Performance by Amateurs are controlled by SAMUEL FRENCH LTD, 26 SOUTHAMPTON STREET, LONDON WC2E 7JE, and they, or their authorized agents, issue licences to amateurs on payment of a fee. **It is an infringement of the Copyright to give any performance or public reading of the play before the fee has been paid and the licence issued.**

Licences are issued subject to the understanding that it shall be made clear in all advertising matter that the audience will witness an amateur performance; that the names of the authors of the plays shall be included on all announcements and on all programmes; and that the integrity of the author's work will be preserved.

The Royalty Fee indicated below is subject to contract and subject to variation at the sole discretion of Samuel French Ltd

> Basic fee for each and every
> performance by amateurs   Code M
> in the British Isles

In Theatres or Halls seating Six Hundred or more the fee will be subject to negotiation.

In Territories Overseas the fee quoted above may not apply. A fee will be quoted on application to our local authorized agent, or if there is no such agent, on application to Samuel French Ltd, London.

The Professional Repertory Rights in this play are controlled by Samuel French Ltd

---

The publication of this play does not imply that it is necessarily available for performance by amateurs or professionals, either in the British Isles or Overseas. Amateurs and professionals considering a production are strongly advised in their own interests to apply to the appropriate agents for consent before starting rehearsals or booking a theatre or hall.

ISBN 0 573 11411 0

SHUT YOUR EYES AND THINK OF ENGLAND

First presented by John Gale at the Apollo Theatre, London, on the 15th November 1977, with the following cast of characters:

Sir Justin Holbrook	Frank Thornton
Stella Richards	Madeline Smith
Arthur Pullen	Donald Sindén
Lady Holbrook	Jan Holden
The Rt Hon. Sir Frederick Goudhurst	Willoughby Goddard
His Highness Sheik Marami	Peter Bland
Mrs Joyce Pullen	Patsy Rowlands
Mr Rubenstein	Ken Wynne
Dr Cornish	Robin Parkinson

The play directed by Patrick Garland

Setting by Peter Rice

The action takes place in a Penthouse Apartment in the City of London

Act I   Early Saturday morning
Act II A few moments later

Time—the present—give or take a Government

The publication of this play in French's Acting Edition must not be taken to imply that it is available for performance. To avoid possible infringement of the copyright please read the fee notice very carefully.

ACT I

A luxury apartment in the City of London overlooking St Paul's. Early morning

The back wall is almost entirely taken up with a picture window with sliding glass doors leading on to a balcony which goes off to one side of the stage. There are four doors in the room: one leading to a bedroom, another to a kitchen, a third to the offices of Holbrook Investments Corporation, and a fourth—double doors—to the hall. This last is the main entrance to the apartment. There is a large sofa in the middle of the room, and some modern gimmicky furniture. The whole impression is that of a high-class business man's pad. The record-player is playing, and the telephone receiver is off its rest

Justin Holbrook enters from the bedroom in his dressing-gown. He is a good-looking well-preserved man in his early fifties. He goes to the sofa table and picks up a dirty brandy glass, then picks up another dirty brandy glass from beside the armchair. He puts both glasses on the drinks cabinet and lifts the record-player lid and turns off the music

Holbrook (*calling*) What do you usually have for breakfast.
Stella (*off*) Just a glass of orange juice.

Stella Richards enters, putting on her wrap, and leans on the bedroom door. She is a very elegant and expensive call-girl

In my game you've got to watch your figure.
Holbrook (*smiling*) Quite.
Stella By the way do you want to pay cash or shall I charge it to your account?
Holbrook I don't really mind, as long as it's confidential.
Stella I should do it on your account. As you know, we call it "secretarial services" and then you can get it off tax as well.
Holbrook Very accommodating. You don't do it on "Diner's Club" yet, do you?
Stella We tried that, but it was such a bore carrying around those heavy machines. (*She sits in the desk chair*) Do you mind if I use the phone to call the Agency?
Holbrook (*putting the receiver back on the phone*) Sure, help yourself.
Stella Oh, you took it off the hook.
Holbrook I have a wife who has a habit of ringing at the most inopportune moments.
Stella I suppose that explains why you don't have one in the bedroom.
Holbrook I don't go in there to make phone calls.

Stella dials

Stella You can say that again.

Holbrook Will there by anyone on duty at this hour? It's only just gone nine. And it is Saturday morning.
Stella We're a genuine twenty-four hour, seven day service.
Holbrook Very commendable.
Stella I like to get my appointments sorted out as early as possible, then I can go home and have a good sleep.
Holbrook That's something we share in common. I'll get your orange juice.

Holbrook exits to the kitchen

Stella (*on the phone*) Morning, Stella Richards here; put me through to Bookings will you... Hello... What's in the diary for me?... Not that American film producer again; he's always asking me to marry him... I keep telling him I don't give complementaries... O.K., six o'clock at his hotel.... Last night? Oh, fine, I think it might become a regular booking...

Holbrook enters with two glasses of orange juice

Yes, he's absolutely charming. 'Bye, call you same time tomorrow. Take care. (*She replaces the receiver*)
Holbrook There you are. (*He gives her a glass*)
Stella Thank you.
Holbrook Who've you got today, anyone I know?
Stella We never discuss one client with another, it's not ethical.
Holbrook I'm glad to hear it.
Stella We're just like your City organizations, secretly efficient.
Holbrook You'd be an asset to any organization. Ever thought of becoming a private secretary?
Stella No, thanks. I tried it once, before I turned professional. Too much like hard work. And all those childish business men chasing you round the filing cabinet. I found it most distasteful.
Holbrook How about another round of pleasure before you go?
Stella Fine by me, but surely you don't want me round when the staff arrive.
Holbrook There's nobody here. The City's closed on a Saturday.
Stella (*looking at a letter on the desk*) By the way, I hope you don't mind my asking, but what exactly is the Holbrook International Investment Corporation? (*She picks up a letter-head*)
Holbrook We're one of the largest private investment institutions in Western Europe. Incidentally we've got a new issue coming up. As Chairman and Managing Director I could always let you in on the ground floor if you're interested.
Stella Thanks, I'll have a word with my stockbroker sometime. Not that I invest much, the tax on unearned income is so crippling these days.
Holbrook You've obviously got a good head for business.
Stella It's all part of the game, isn't it? And of course I use the best firm of chartered accountants!
Holbrook Of course!
Stella They assure me I'm sitting on a fortune!
Holbrook I see their point. Come on!

Act I

Stella rises. She and Holbrook move to the bedroom door

   Stella exits to the bedroom

There is a tapping on the office door

   (*Surprised*) What the devil ...

He hastily closes the bedroom door. There is another tentative tap. He goes to the desk and collects the glasses of orange juice

   Coming! (*He goes to the drinks cabinet and puts the glasses on it, then moves to the main door and opens it*)

   Arthur Pullen enters with briefcase, umbrella, spectacles, bowler hat and mac. He is a punctilious accountant in his late forties

Pullen Sir Justin, I hope I'm not intruding?
Holbrook Pullen, what the hell are you doing here?
Pullen Well, I caught the early train, the eight oh-nine from Coulsdon South, getting into London Bridge at eight thirty-six. Coulsdon South is a bit further from my home than Coulsdon North but it's a much faster service, and anyway the trains from Coulsdon North stop at every station and don't run at all on Saturdays.
Holbrook (*blankly*) Ah.
Pullen And I wanted to be here by eight fifty, and was. Normally, of course, I get the eight nineteen which gets me in promptly at eight forty-two and then it's only a brisk eight-minute walk. There are those occasions, however, when we're all diverted to Victoria.

Holbrook moves into the room. Pullen follows him

Holbrook I didn't ask for a detailed run down on the Southern Region, I want to know why you're here on a Saturday.
Pullen To finish the books, ready for audit. I'm going on holiday today. I got here early, so that I could leave at three and I've brought sandwiches for lunch, so I shall have plenty of time to polish the job off.
Holbrook Well, get on with it. Why the hell are you knocking on my door?
Pullen The Office Manager isn't here today and he forgot to give me the appropriate keys. And I've been twiddling my thumbs for nearly ten minutes wondering what to do. Then suddenly it occurred to me that you might be staying the night in the penthouse, recovering from your Far East flight yesterday before joining your wife in the country today.
Holbrook Get to the point, Pullen.
Pullen The cabinet keys.

Holbrook goes to the desk, opens the drawer and gets the keys. Pullen goes to take the keys from Holbrook and leaves his briefcase on the desk

Holbrook The way you waffle round in circles, Pullen, I sometimes wonder how you ever became such a good accountant.
Pullen Thank you, sir.
Holbrook (*gives him the keys*) That wasn't meant to be a compliment.

Pullen (*laughing*) Oh, I see. Thank you, sir.
Holbrook Go away, Pullen.

Pullen goes to the main doors

    Oh, Pullen, use my door to the office. That door!

Pullen goes to the office door

    And don't forget to return the keys.

Pullen steps to Holbrook

Pullen No, sir.
Holbrook And, Pullen ...

Holbrook goes to the armchair. Pullen moves to him

Pullen Sir?
Holbrook Have a nice holiday.
Pullen Thank you, sir.

Pullen steps to the office door, then back to Holbrook

    It'll be Bournemouth of course again this year. Joyce, my wife that is, does so enjoy it there, and they're used to us now at the Palace Court, and ...

Holbrook I'm glad somebody's used to you, for goodness' sake get out!
Pullen Yes.

Pullen exits to the office, then re-enters immediately

    Don't worry, I shall be back on the fourteenth ...
Holbrook I can't wait!

Pullen exits to the office, slamming the door. He re-enters

Pullen I'm sorry, sir. I slammed the door.

Pullen exits to the office. Stella enters as Holbrook locks the office door and takes the key out

Stella What's the matter—gone off the idea?
Holbrook Of course not. But one of my staff's turned up.
Stella Oh no! Perhaps I'd better go then.

Holbrook goes and shuts the main doors and moves to the sofa.

Holbrook No, it's no-one of any importance, only Pullen, he's the accountant going on holiday—came in early from Coulsdon North, I mean South—going to Bournemouth—I don't mean he's going to Bournemouth from Coulsdon ... (*stops*) He'll have us all at it next.

Stella and Holbrook exit to the bedroom, leaving the door open. Pullen knocks on the office door and unlocks it with the key and enters

Pullen Sorry to disturb you ...

Act I

Seeing no-one there, Pullen goes to the desk. Stella and Holbrook laugh from the bedroom. Pullen steps to the bedroom, then goes to the desk, picks up his briefcase, and moves to the office door. There is more laughter from the bedroom. Pullen is rooted to the spot. There is a thud from the bedroom

Stella (*off*) Sir Justin, Sir Justin! What's the matter? Are you all right?

Stella enters from the bedroom

Doctor! Doctor!
Pullen I'm not a doctor. I work here.
Stella You're Mr Pullen?
Pullen Er—er—er ...
Stella Well, are you?
Pullen Yes.
Stella Then ring for a doctor. I think something's happened to my client.
Pullen Your client?
Stella Sir Justin Holbrook. I think he's had a heart attack in the middle.
Pullen In the middle?
Stella In the middle of the bedroom.
Pullen Good Lord.
Stella Are you going to dial or shall I?
Pullen Dial?
Stella For an ambulance—get him to hospital.
Pullen But they might take him to a public ward in the East End. He should go West.
Stella He will if we don't hurry.

Stella goes to the desk and dials. Pullen goes to the bedroom door and looks through

Pullen It's all right, he's still moving.
Stella D'you think one of us should give him the kiss of life?
Pullen I imagine you'd be better at it than I.
Stella (*on the phone*) Oh yes, ambulance, hold on!

Stella gives the phone to Pullen and moves to the bedroom door

You deal with them. I'll see what I can do to help in there.

Stella rushes into the bedroom

Pullen takes the phone and puts the keys on the desk

Pullen (*on the phone*) Emergency. My name is Pullen, Arthur Pullen ... I'm the accountant ... no, I'm not the patient. Well, it's for my Chairman, Sir Justin Holbrook, I think it might be a heart attack ... Where am I? I'm standing by the desk in the lounge ... Ah! The Holbrook International Investment Corporation, two hundred and twenty Gracechurch Street, London EC three one JW ... Oh, on a go-slow? But this is an emergency ... Well, do the best you can, after all he is on BUPA ... Well, it's like the A.A., isn't it? You can be towed in for nothing ...

Stella and Holbrook enter from the bedroom. Holbrook is draped in a blanket

Stella Are they on their way?
Pullen I wouldn't bank on it. (*He looks up*) Good Lord.

Stella and Holbrook sit on the sofa

(*On the phone*) This girl kissed him ...
Holbrook Pullen!
Pullen I mean I kissed him—well somebody kissed him and he's come to life so you can put your ambulance away. (*He replaces the receiver*) I must say I'm delighted to see you've recovered.
Holbrook Thank you.
Stella Are you sure you're all right now?
Holbrook Yes, yes, it was just a temporary black-out.
Pullen The "bends"?
Holbrook I beg your pardon?
Pullen The sort of thing experienced by divers and astronauts when they're going down or coming up.
Holbrook Quite. It's a nervous condition of the heart, called Stokes-Adams syndrome.
Stella You won't be needing me again, will you?
Holbrook Not in the immediate future, no.

Stella kisses Holbrook on the forehead. Pullen looks away

Stella exits to the bedroom

Pullen goes to the desk, collects his briefcase and moves to the sofa

Pullen (*tactfully*) Charming young lady. Bit of luck she was here really to give it to you.
Holbrook Give me what?
Pullen The—kiss of life.
Holbrook Wait a minute, Pullen, I seem to remember locking that door.
Pullen You did sir, but I had to come back for my briefcase. It contained my sandwiches and coffee, and as you kindly gave me the keys I used them to re-enter. I was on the point of going out again when I heard a cry of distress and your "mas–", "mas–"—er, physiotherapist came rushing in.
Holbrook Don't be so damned diplomatic, you know exactly what she is, and what we were doing.
Pullen Well, if I did, I would never—and I won't!
Holbrook Not if you value your job.
Pullen Oh, I do.
Holbrook I dare say you've had one or two mild peccadilloes in your time.
Pullen Mild what, sir?
Holbrook A bit on the side.
Pullen Oh, I see. Well, I wouldn't deny it's crossed my mind from time to time, but there's not a lot of scope for it in Coulsdon.
Holbrook Well, you've not in Coulsdon now. (*He gives him a wink*) You're

Act I 7

on the loose in the big city and I'm sure if you feel like having a word with Miss Richards ...
Pullen (*covered with embarrassment*) Oh, I couldn't, sir, and anyway it's too soon after breakfast. (*He goes to the office door*)
Holbrook Go on.
Pullen No, really.
Holbrook It's on the house, Pullen.
Pullen (*moving back*) You mean the firm's paying for this?
Holbrook Of course, you should know, you've been making out the cheques all these years. "Mount Street Secretarial Agency."
Pullen (*appalled*) But they run out at thousands of pounds a month.
Holbrook So?
Pullen Good Lord, I don't wonder you have black-outs.
Holbrook They're not all for me, you idiot, there's the entire board of directors and overseas investors. For instance, you'd be surprised how insatiable the Rotarians are.
Pullen But we're a public company, quoted on the Stock Exchange. Some of the biggest institutions in the City invest with us.
Holbrook And how d'you think we got them to invest in the first place?
Pullen Presumably because they think we're a sound company.
Holbrook Sound companies are two a penny. So we have to offer the investment managers a bonus, you know, a little "something" for themselves.
Pullen (*aghast*) A little "something"—you don't mean "inducements"?
Holbrook Certainly.
Pullen Supposing somebody found out?
Holbrook Fortunately we in the City are men of honour. We exist on trust.
Pullen That's all very well, but I mean supposing a rival company got wind of these activities?
Holbrook "Let him who is without sin cast the first stone."
Pullen D'you mean that other companies indulge in ...
Holbrook This square mile isn't the financial capital of the world for nothing. And we're in a very competitive market.
Pullen One might almost say "shady".
Holbrook One better not, Pullen.

Holbrook rises and moves to the desk. Pullen follows

You never know when there might be a City editor lurking in a wine bar.
Pullen Oh, I don't frequent such places. As you know, I bring my sandwiches and a thermos flask of coffee—even soup sometimes. Joyce prepares it all whilst I'm having breakfast, unless of course I'm catching a very early train, like today, in which case she does it the night before ...
Holbrook Spare me the homely details and get me a glass of water. (*He gets a bottle of pills from the desk drawer and takes one*)
Pullen Yes, of course, at once. (*He goes to the drinks cabinet and pours a glass of water*) It's all been a bit of a shock.
Holbrook Don't worry, these little attacks of mine look worse than they are.
Pullen You misunderstand me, sir.

Pullen gives Holbrook the glass of water. Holbrook takes his pills

I didn't mean the state of your health, I meant the state of the company. You must appreciate that as a company accountant I'm in a very invidious position. How can I possibly live with the knowledge that I'm dealing with tainted money?

Holbrook Don't be so pi, Pullen (*He goes to the drinks cabinet and pours a whisky*) You're not handling the Boy Scout kitty.

Pullen I've been a party to fiscal chicanery.

Holbrook Balderdash. Tell you what, pop your Bournemouth bill on to expenses when you get back.

Pullen That won't solve anything, sir.

Holbrook Have a rise in salary as well.

Pullen That won't do any good either.

Holbrook (*moving to Pullen*) That's my final offer, you're not going to blackmail me.

Pullen Blackmail? You don't think I'm after money, do you?

Holbrook What the hell *do* you want?

Pullen I want all this to stop before it's too late.

Holbrook What are you trying to do, ruin us?

Pullen I just want everything to be honest and above-board.

Holbrook You must be mad. We'd be the laughing stock of the market. You're sure you wouldn't like me to give all my money away to charity? (*He sits on the sofa*)

Pullen Not all of it, only the tainted part.

Holbrook You'd better start donating your *own* salary, it all comes from the same source.

Pullen But I didn't know that.

Holbrook Well, you know it now.

Pullen I'm sorry, Sir Justin, I think in the circumstances I have no alternative but to tender my resignation. (*He picks up his briefcase, moves to the main doors and opens them*)

Holbrook In that case I have no alternative but to ring the police and have you arrested.

Pullen steps back and shuts the main doors

Pullen What on earth for? I haven't done anything.

Holbrook Yes, you have, you've been countersigning the cheques for years.

Pullen But I'm innocent.

Holbrook Just try proving it. What are they going to think when I tell them you were here at nine o'clock on a Saturday morning, cooking the books with a naked girl? That'll go down well in Coulsdon.

Pullen (*moving to the sofa*) You wouldn't do a thing like that, sir?

Holbrook I would if I had to. My first loyalty is to my shareholders. They're quite satisfied with the way I'm looking after their money.

Pullen But they don't know *how* you're looking after it.

Holbrook That's why they're satisfied. Now you must excuse me. (*He rises*) That tablet seems to be working now, I feel a lot better.

Pullen I feel a lot worse.

Stella enters; she is now dressed, but is in her stocking feet and carries an overnight bag

Stella Anybody seen my shoes?

Pullen and Holbrook look for her shoes

Holbrook Down there.

Stella puts her overnight bag on the sofa. Pullen picks up the shoes from under the armchair and puts his briefcase on the armchair. Holbrook takes the shoes from Pullen. Stella goes to Holbrook, who gives her the shoes

There you are, my dear.
Stella Oh, thanks.

Stella sits on the sofa and puts on her shoes. Pullen gazes at her shapely legs

You all right now?
Holbrook Yes, thank you, it was really nothing.
Stella Good. I've so enjoyed my visit, such a change when you're able to combine business with business.
Holbrook (*jokingly to Pullen*) Quite sure you wouldn't like to go over the Mount Street Secretarial figure?
Pullen (*flustered*) Please, Sir Justin—er, no offence to this young lady of course.
Stella Don't worry, Mr Pullen, another time. (*She moves to Pullen*) During your lunch break perhaps?
Pullen No, no, you see I have sandwiches instead—I mean instead of going out. Then if I *do* feel the need for exercise I can always take a stroll. Not that I'm looking a gift horse in the mouth—I don't mean horse, I mean a most attractive young mare—filly—er ...
Holbrook Pullen, you're beginning to aggravate my condition. (*He puts the glass on the sofa table*)
Pullen I'm so sorry—yes, forgive me, shall I retire?
Holbrook I wish you would, permanently.
Pullen I couldn't do that. I'd have to sell my house in Coulsdon.
Holbrook Out!
Pullen (*backing out with his briefcase*) Yes, quite, I'm so sorry.

Pullen exists to the office, shutting the door

Stella Poor little man, we shouldn't tease him. Sure you're going to be all right now?
Holbrook Perfectly. By the way, how about giving me your home number?
Stella Oh no, sorry, all bookings strictly through the Agency. It's more than my life's worth to accept private work on the side.
Holbrook It's just that I thought we might arrange something on a more regular basis.
Stella I'll tell you what. I'll get the Agency to send you a leaflet on contract hire. But you realize you'll have to pay ten months in advance.

Holbrook Good heavens.
Stella Don't blame us, it's the law.
Holbrook And how do they invoice that? Office equipment?
Stella No, bedding.

They exchange a quick kiss and then part as the main door opens

Lady Valerie Holbrook enters; she is elegant and sophisticated

Valerie Darling, I was trying to ring all last night but ... (*She stops in her tracks as she sees Stella*) I thought so.
Holbrook Valerie, my angel, before you jump to ...
Valerie (*controlling herself*) Don't you angel me. (*To Stella*) I wonder if you'd be so kind as to get the hell out of here.
Stella If you insist.
Holbrook Wait. Darling, I would ask you not to speak like that to the wife of one of my most valued employees.
Valerie (*moving to Holbrook*) I could almost tolerate the occasional tart, but if you're going to start on other men's wives ...
Holbrook You're making a complete fool of yourself, dear. This lady has only just arrived.
Valerie At nine o'clock in the morning?
Holbrook She arrived with her husband. Allow me to introduce you. You've never met Mrs Pullen, have you?
Valerie Yes, at the Annual Dinner-Dance, rather a dumpy woman in purple satin, she nagged her husband most of the evening.
Holbrook Yes, that was the start of it, the divorce, went through a terrible time, poor chap. But I'm delighted to say he's re-married now to the—er—the second Mrs Pullen.
Stella How do you do, Lady Holbrook.
Valerie (*still a little suspicious*) How do you do. You must be a lot younger than your husband.
Stella (*sweetly*) Thank you. May I return the compliment.
Valerie (*still not quite convinced*) Yes, you may! Is that overnight bag yours?
Stella Er—yes.
Holbrook (*quickly*) Yes, Mr and Mrs Pullen are off to Bournemouth on their holiday. Such a conscientious fellow, he's insisted on coming in today to get the books up to date before he goes, brought his sandwiches, and Mrs Pullen is going to do a little last-minute shopping.
Valerie I didn't know there were any shops open in the City on a Saturday.
Holbrook You're absolutely right. She's going on to the West End. They came up on the eight oh-nine from Coulsdon South and it was just when they arrived at the office that it happened.
Valerie What happened?
Holbrook I had one of my black-outs.
Valerie Darling!
Holbrook Very lucky they were here, wasn't it?
Stella Yes. We started to phone for an ambulance, but fortunately I was able to give the kiss of life.

Act I

Valerie Indeed?
Holbrook She's a nurse.
Valerie Which hospital?
Holbrook (*to Stella*) I'm not sure. It is Bart's or Guys?
Stella I'm with an agency.
Holbrook She's with an agen ... Yes, well. She trained with Guy's—for guys—at Guy's.

Pullen enters from the office

Trying not to be seen, he goes to the desk, collects the keys, then moves back towards the door

Pullen Sorry to intrude, but I left my keys on the ... (*Startled*) Lady Holbrook!
Valerie Good morning, Mr Pullen.
Pullen What a shock—er, shocking memory I have. I'm always forgetting something. (*He shows them the keys*)
Valerie I was very glad to hear from my husband that you've come through all your troubles.
Pullen Troubles?
Holbrook (*pointedly*) Domestic troubles.
Valerie With your wife.
Pullen My wife?
Holbrook Your first wife. Not the second Mrs Pullen to whom you're so happily married now.

Holbrook indicates Stella. Pullen turns and looks at Stella, then back at Holbrook—then "double-takes" on Stella

Pullen Christmas!
Stella Yes, Christmas, don't you remember? (*Hastily taking his arm*) That's when we were married, at Christmas. And you said I was the nicest Christmas present you'd ever had.
Pullen You would be—wouldn't you? She was. Wasn't she?
Valerie I suppose your holiday in Bournemouth is a sort of second honeymoon.
Pullen Sort of, yes.
Valerie (*to Holbrook*) I think it's time you got dressed, Justin, you can hardly walk around like that all day.
Holbrook Right, just give me a moment. (*He suffers another relapse*) Ah! (*He faints on the sofa*)
Valerie (*rushing to help him*) Poor thing, he's been overdoing it.
Pullen Indeed he has.
Valerie Nurse!
Pullen What?
Valerie Nurse!
Pullen Good idea, I'll go out and get one.
Valerie Don't be stupid, Mr Pullen, your wife's here.
Pullen Where? (*He looks round the room*)
Valerie There. She's a nurse, isn't she?

Pullen Er ...
Stella Yes of course I am.
Pullen Yes of course she is.
Stella Let's get him into the bedroom.
Pullen No, give him the kiss of life.

Stella kneels on the sofa and breathes into Holbrook. Then she lies on top of Holbrook still kissing him. Pullen and Valerie look away, embarrassed

(*Hastily*) It's the standard technique, very effective, especially with male patients.

Holbrook comes round. Stella sits on the sofa and Holbrook clings to her. Pullen tries to part Holbrook and Stella

Holbrook (*faintly*) Oh, Miss Richard ...
Valerie Miss ... What?
Pullen Says he feels wretched.
Stella Let's get him on to the bed.

Pullen gets Stella's overnight bag and puts it by bedroom door

Valerie No, no, he's much better sitting up. Let's keep him on the sofa. Nurse, put the blanket round him.

Stella puts the blanket round Holbrook and then sits on the floor

Sir Frederick Goudhurst enters from the main doors with walking-stick, briefcase and hat. He is an imposing senior civil servant

Sir Frederick Forgive me calling on you so early in the day.
Valerie Quite all right, Freddie.
Sir Frederick (*moving to the sofa*) What's happened?
Valerie I'm afraid poor Justin has had one of his attacks!
Sir Frederick Nothing serious, I hope.
Valerie No, just a nervous condition.
Holbrook I'll be all right, Goudhurst, do please sit down.
Sir Frederick Have you called a doctor?
Valerie No need. Anyway, luckily there was a nurse here.
Holbrook Pullen, look after Sir Frederick.
Pullen (*very deferentially*) Of course, do please sit down, Sir Frederick. May I take your hat and stick.
Sir Frederick Thank you.

Pullen takes Sir Frederick's hat, briefcase and stick. Sir Frederick sits in the armchair

Pullen Some refreshment perhaps? A cup of coffee, or it may be soup.
Sir Frederick No, I've just had a working breakfast at Claridge's, which, incidentally, is why I'm here now. Is there any chance of us being left alone, Justin?
Holbrook I'm afraid in my present state I'd feel happier if everyone remained. my wife, my nurse and my accountant.

Act I

Pullen Oh no—sir—I ...
Holbrook Whom I've just appointed my chief accountant!
Pullen (*visibly blossoming*) Oh—sir, I—I—I—I—I'm speechless.
Holbrook I'm glad to hear it. Now then, Freddie. What's happened?
Sir Frederick I've just spent the most nerve-racking time in the V.I.P. suite with His Highness Sheik Marami.
Pullen (*impressed*) Good Lord.
Holbrook Didn't know he was in the country.
Sir Frederick Nor does anyone else, apart from the P.M. and the Chancellor of the Exchequer. It's top secret. We've had a week of very tough financial negotiations. I must impress upon you to keep this matter confidential.
Pullen We will, we will, you can be absolutely sure of that, sir. I won't even discuss it with my wife on the train to Bournemouth, five thirty from Waterloo—full dining service, we shall probably have tea and biscuits, gets the holiday off to a good start.
Holbrook Oh, shut up, Pullen! Go on, Freddie?
Sir Frederick Marami is threatening to pull out all his money from this country.
Holbrook Oh my God. What about the rest of the Arab countries?
Sir Frederick They'll follow his lead, pull out their millions as well.
Holbrook The country would collapse. The City'll be finished.
Pullen Britain could go broke.

Pullen puts Sir Frederick's hat on the top of the hi-fi, and the briefcase and walking-stick by main doors

Sir Frederick Precisely, it would wipe thousands of millions off the Stock Market in a matter of minutes.
Pullen Worse than the Wall Street Crash.
Stella But why?
Sir Frederick My dear girl, this country is working on borrowed money, borrowed time and massive Middle East investments.
Stella The Arabs have certainly helped to boost our going rates.
Holbrook Yes. (*Hastily*) In the private nursing field.
Sir Frederick And they like the way we in the City of London take care of their money as well. We're still the foremost international money market, but frankly it's only thanks to the Arabs in general and Marami in particular.
Holbrook (*rising*) What's he after exactly?
Sir Frederick He wants majority control of this company.
Holbrook The devil he does! (*He goes and sits at the desk*)
Pullen The Holbrook International Investment Corporation?
Sir Frederick Yes.
Pullen But we're the biggest and most respected in the City.
Sir Frederick Exactly. Unfortunately he's lost patience with this government. But I've come up with a rather ingenious compromise solution.
Pullen Well done, sir.
Sir Frederick I've persuaded him ours is the only investment company he can trust to handle his financial affairs.

Holbrook I've never met Sheik Marami.
Sir Frederick No, but he's had his spies out and he realizes the extent of our operations. He knows all the leading financial institutions invest with us.
Pullen Most of the big Insurance Companies and Unit Trusts.
Sir Frederick Public Companies.
Pullen Nationalized Industries.
Sir Frederick London Boroughs.
Pullen Trade Unions.
Holbrook Shut up, Pullen. Freddie, what's the attitude of Downing Street, the Treasury and the Bank of England?
Sir Frederick They're not very happy about it, it's a pistol at our heads. It's either that or the country faces virtual collapse. So we've got to sign everything before Marami flies home at mid-day.
Pullen You can't do that. The Articles of our company dictate that we call a shareholders' meeting.
Holbrook He's right.
Sir Frederick There's no time. Marami and his lawyer are on their way here now!
Holbrook What, here?
Pullen This morning?
Sir Frederick Yes, but as you and I own fifty-one per cent of the shares, we've got control. And here's the twist, our friend the Sheik won't pay one penny over par!
Holbrook But that would ruin me! Ah!

Holbrook faints on the desk and pushes the phone on to the floor. Valerie, Pullen and Stella gather round him

Valerie Justin—Justin ... (*To Sir Frederick*) Now look what you've done!
Sir Frederick I'm awfully sorry.
Valerie Nurse, what do we do?
Stella Ring for a doctor, I think he's become immune to my kisses.
Sir Frederick (*rising*) Someone's got to bring him round, and quickly, or we'll *all* need a doctor.
Valerie (*trying to revive Holbrook*) Justin, it's me, speak to me ...
Pullen Shall I take his pulse?
Valerie No, get on the phone, call his doctor.
Pullen Yes. (*He goes to pick up the phone*)
Valerie D'you know his name? (*She picks up the desk phone book*)
Pullen (*without thinking*) Yes. Sir Justin Holbrook.
Valerie The doctor's.
Pullen No.
Valerie Fosgrove in Harley Street. Five-eight-oh double-oh-three-four.
Pullen Five-eight-oh double-oh-three-four, right. (*He writes the number on a pad and picks up the "trick" phone from above the desk*)
Valerie Nurse, get him a glass of water; we'll try and get a tablet down him.

Stella exits to the kitchen

Act I

Sir Frederick Anything I can do?
Valerie I think you've done enough already.
Sir Frederick Yes, well, get on with it, man.

Pullen pulls the top cover off the phone and puts it in the waste-paper bin. He starts to dial, as the dial falls off, but is still attached by wires. He puts the receiver in between his legs and uses both hands to dial

Valerie Pullen, what are you doing with that phone?
Pullen (*trying to shove the "intestines" of the phone back into place*) It's a little difficult. I've managed to dial, but I'm not sure the rest of it's working ... Ah! Success. (*Into the phone*) Hello, is that Dr Fosgrove's surgery? ... Oh good, this is Arthur Pullen speaking ... Accountant, Chief Accountant, actually. I'm speaking on behalf of Sir Justin Holbrook, I think he has had a heart attack. Could the doctor come as soon as possible? ... He's where? ... In his car ... Oh, I can reach him there, can I? (*To the others in wonderment*) He's got a phone in his car!

Stella enters with a glass of water

Stella and Valerie try to get the tablet down Holbrook

I could never see the point of them till now. Always thought it was rather ostentatious.
Sir Frederick Get the number!
Pullen Yes.

The mouthpiece cover falls off and the microphone hangs from the receiver by wires. He lifts the mouthpiece to his lips

(*On the phone*) What's the number, please? ... I'm sorry, you'll have to speak louder, the innards have fallen out ... No, the innards of the phone ... (*To the others*) Slight misunderstanding, she thought I was referring to Sir Justin.
Sir Frederick What's the number!
Pullen (*on the phone*) Sorry, could you repeat that, please ... Dial one-four-oh for the operator. Yes, and one-nine what?
Valerie We're never going to get this tablet down him. (*She puts the glass and pill on the desk*)
Sir Frederick Is he still unconscious?
Stella I'm afraid so.
Pullen Hello, operator, I want Dr Fosgrove in his car, one-nine-one-two-three.
Valerie He should've come straight home last night from the airport.
Sir Frederick Just as well he didn't. I could never have got to your country house in time, and made it back here to sign with Marami.
Pullen (*on the phone*) Hello ... (*To the others*) Ah, success. (*On the phone*) Dr Fosgrove? ... Is that you in your car? ... I'm ringing on behalf of ... Oh, very well, I'll hold on.
Valerie Now what's the matter?

Pullen Would you believe it, he's on his other line ... (*Listening*) Packet of Cornflakes—three tins of Kit-E-Kat ... He's giving his grocery order.
Sir Frederick Give it to me. (*He goes to Pullen, grabs the phone and gets entangled in the flex*)
Pullen Be careful, sir.
Sir Frederick Idiot. (*He disentangles himself, leaves the phone to Pullen, and turns to Holbrook*) Don't worry, old chap. Help is on its way.
Valerie He can't hear you.
Sir Frederick It could be that he's only lost the power of speech. It's not uncommon, you know.
Pullen Yes, my wife had an aunt once, who lived in Shirley—no, I tell a lie, her name was Shirley and she lived in Croydon, or was it Penge.
Sir Frederick Stop babbling, Pullen. (*He sits on the sofa*)
Valerie (*to Stella*) Does your husband always go on like this?
Stella I don't know.
Valerie What do you mean, "you don't know"?
Stella I mean I haven't seen a lot of him. He's at work all day and I'm out all night—on duty.
Valerie I don't blame you.
Pullen (*on the phone*, Dr Fosgrove, where are you now? ... In a traffic jam, oh dear. (*To the others*) He's nose to bumper in Piccadilly.
Sir Frederick Ask him what we should do till he gets here.
Pullen (*on the phone*) Dr Fosgrove, where are you now? ... In a traffic jam, treatment? ... Yes, as far as we know it's a recurrence of his usual trouble ...
Valerie Tell him your wife's here and she's a nurse.
Pullen (*on the phone*) Apparently your wife's here and she's a nurse. (*Realizing his mistake*) Oh, my wife's the nurse ... Tell her what? ... Yes I will, thank you, Doctor. (*He puts the phone down*)
Valerie What did he say?
Pullen He said it's a Stokes-Adams attack. Get him to bed and you'll know what to do.
Valerie (*to Stella*) What is Stokes-Adams?
Stella How should I know?
Valerie But you're a nurse.
Stella Look, I think it's about time I told you that I'm not a ...
Pullen (*jumping in quickly*) Not an ordinary nurse, an animal nurse, a vet.
Sir Frederick She just said she was on night duty.
Pullen That's right. Works for the R.S.P.C.A. drives around in a van all night picking up stray dogs and cats and hamsters.

Valerie goes to Holbrook and pushes Stella away

Valerie Then you get away from my husband, you might give him mange.
Pullen How dare you treat Miss ... (*He moves to Stella*) Mrs Pullen like that. (*He takes hold of Stella protectively*) She's only trying to help.
Stella Thank you, Arthur.
Pullen (*beginning to realize he could be on to a good thing*) God, you're stunning.

Act I   17

Sir Frederick Why's he talking to her like that? She's his wife.
Valerie Second wife, they've only been married a few months.
Sir Frederick Lucky fellow, at your age. Tell me, what's the secret of your fatal charm?
Pullen Modesty forbids.
Valerie Look, could we pursue the secret of your marital success some other time, and concentrate on getting my husband back to bed?
Pullen Certainly. (*He gets the blanket from the sofa and gives it to Stella*) Stella, my love, would you take that (*He kisses Stella*)

Stella exits to the bedroom

And, Lady Holbrook, if you could take most of the weight ...

Pullen helps Valerie to get Holbrook up

Holbrook and Valerie exit to the bedroom. Pullen follows

The telephone rings. Sir Frederick rises and answers it

Sir Frederick (*on the phone*) Hellow, Goudhurst here ... Oh hello, Chancellor ... No, I haven't managed to get anything signed yet. Holbrook's been taken ill ... No, he's still in the office but out for the count. We've got hold of his doctor and he's on the way ... Yes, as soon as I have any news I'll let you know ...

Sheik Marami enters from the main doors, shuts them, and moves to Sir Frederick. He is in full Arab clothes

Sir Frederick puts the phone down hastily

Your Highness, I'm afraid your arrival is a trifle premature. For technical reasons we haven't been able to complete our business yet.
Marami I understood it was merely a question of obtaining the signature of Sir Justin Holbrook.
Sir Frederick That's quite right, yes.
Marami There are no problems, are there?
Sir Frederick No, nothing insurmountable.
Marami He has agreed then? (*He sits in the armchair*)
Sir Frederick Yes, he saw the wisdom of the whole thing right away. (*He sits on the sofa*) It's just that I caught him at an awkward moment.
Marami How so?
Sir Frederick He was in bed.
Marami Sleeping? (*He looks at his watch*)
Sir Frederick No, he's in bed with Stokes-Adams.
Marami (*smiling*) Well, I hope they are enjoying themselves.
Sir Frederick No, you don't understand, he's got a complaint.
Marami Then he should kick this Stokes-Adams out of the bed and find someone else.
Sir Frederick It's a sickness.
Marami Not in my country, we recognize all types of relationship. And so,

if I may say so, did your great T. E. Lawrence. My uncle knew him, intimately. I suppose this Adams is from the Foreign Office.
Sir Frederick Allow me to clarify matters.
Marami No need. I know what goes in these circles.

Pullen enters from the bedroom

Pullen I don't like the look of him, he's still very queer.
Marami Ah, then you are the Stokes-Adams.
Pullen No, he's in there.
Marami Ah, then you are Sir Justin.
Pullen What?

Sir Frederick and Marami rise

Sir Frederick Of course, forgive me, Your Highness, you haven't met, have you?
Marami Not until now. But I'm sure we can look forward to a long and prosperous relationship from now on, can't we?
Pullen Can we?
Sir Frederick We certainly can. (*Introducing them*) His Highness Sheik Marami, allow me to present Sir Justin Holbrook.
Marami Greetings. (*He extends his hand*)
Pullen Actually I—I—I ...
Sir Frederick (*aside*) Come on, old chap, take his hand.

Pullen goes and shakes Marami's hand

Pullen Sheik—er, how do you do?
Marami I'm delighted to make your acquaintance, Sir Justin.
Pullen And I—me—yours. Little did I know when I got up this morning who I'd be.
Marami Pardon?
Pullen Who I'd be meeting.
Marami You seem somewhat nervous, Sir Justin.
Pullen I must admit I'm not quite myself.
Sir Frederick Just a spot of jet-lag. He flew in last night, from Johannesburg.
Marami You should take a holiday.
Pullen As a matter of fact, my wife and I are off this afternoon to Bournemouth.
Sir Frederick (*cutting in*) Borneo.
Marami Borneo?
Pullen Borneo?
Sir Frederick Combined holiday and business trip. He's buying up all the rubber plantations.
Marami That is good news. Your financial empire is expanding faster than I thought. So by noon today I shall have added all this wealth to my millions (*He moves up and opens the window*) I shall not only have Westminster, but the City of London at my feet. I shall rename this building Marami House. We'll make the Barbican into a bazaar and it occurs to me that St Paul's might convert admirably into a mosque.

Act I

Marami walks out on to the balcony to survey his kingdom and goes off out of sight

Pullen (*appalled*) What are you doing?
Sir Frederick Sh! (*He pulls him to one side*) The country's on the verge of collapse and, God help us, you're the only man who can save it.
Pullen How?
Sir Frederick You've got to be Sir Justin, only for this morning, and sign everything I put in front of you.
Pullen That's forgery and false pretences.
Sir Frederick And furthermore, you're married to Valerie Holbrook not Stella.
Pullen That's bigamy.
Sir Frederick And you're lumbered with Stokes-Adams as well.
Pullen There's nothing the matter with my heart.
Sir Frederick Yes there is, you're in love with Stokes-Adams.
Pullen In love with it?
Sir Frederick Not *it*—him. (*He points to Marami outside*) He thinks he's your boyfriend.

Pullen jumps on to the top steps in horror

Pullen I refuse to shack up with a Sheik.
Sir Frederick No Stokes-Adams. Marami thinks you're Holbrook, married of course to Lady Holbrook, but also having an affair with a man called Stokes-Adams from the Foreign Office.
Pullen It's all so confusing. Why do I have to be a homo—homo—
Sir Frederick For Queen and Country.

Pullen goes to the main doors as if to leave

Pullen I don't think I can go through with it.
Sir Frederick Not even for a knighthood?
Pullen (*stopping dead*) A knighthood? "Sir Arthur ...?" (*He steps back and pulls himself to his full height*)
Sir Frederick These things can be arranged, you know.
Pullen (*savouring it*) "Sir Arthur Pullen".
Sir Frederick But you and I have got to save this country first.
Pullen Very well. (*He moves to Sir Frederick*)

Marami enters from the balcony

I'll do my best, but I must catch the five thirty to Bourne ... (*He sees Marami entering*) to Borneo.
Marami The vista from my balcony here will be magnificent once I have redeveloped the area.
Sir Frederick You're planning to redevelop the City?
Marami Certainly, it is all part of my master plan.
Pullen But we've only just had it done.
Marami Not very well, if I may say so. There are still too many old buildings and the streets are pitifully narrow, my Cadillacs might get scratched.

Pullen Some of this architecture goes back a thousand years.
Marami Compared with the Pyramids, jerry building.

Marami takes Pullen's arm and moves to the sofa

I have it in mind to put you in charge of my whole building scheme Sir Justin.
Pullen That's very kind of you, but I'm hardly qualified, Your Highness.
Marami You're too modest. I'm sure you and your friend Stokes-Adams have a highly developed artistic flair, the two generally go hand in hand.
Sir Frederick (*pointedly*) Yes, they do.
Pullen Oh—(*coyly*)—only in private.
Marami Please don't disguise your natural inclinations because of me, feel free to be your gay self.
Sir Frederick Yes, go on, Justin, be gay.

Pullen dithers with embarrassment and finally he tentatively puts his hand on his hip

Pullen (*to Marami*) What a dear thing you are.
Marami That's better.
Pullen I like your frock.
Marami Very good. (*He chuckles*)
Sir Frederick I think we'd better get on with the signing.
Pullen Yes, then we can all have a party. (*He gives a gay little skip*)

Marami sits in the armchair

Sir Frederick You've brought the documents, have you, Marami?
Marami No, my London lawyer is preparing them now and I've told Mr Rubenstein to bring them here.
Sir Frederick Did you say Rubenstein?
Marami Of Rubenstein and Gold, a small but efficient firm in Cricklewood.
Pullen They sound as if they could be Jewish to me.
Marami They are.
Pullen How quaint.
Marami You don't think I'd trust an Arab lawyer. Besides he's cheap and he works on a Saturday.

The phone rings

Sir Frederick Your phone is ringing, Sir Justin.

Pullen goes to the desk and picks up the phone. Sir Frederick sits on the sofa

Pullen (*on the phone*) Hello ... Ah, Dr Fosgrove, good of you to call ... Yes, I think he's holding his own. Where are you now? ... Crawling along Fleet Street ... A burst water main ... Get here as soon as you can. I think the Stokes-Adams attack is under control. Good-bye. (*He replaces the receiver*)
Marami Stokes-Adams has attacked someone?
Sir Frederick (*quietly*) Oh, God.
Marami Who is the victim of this Adams' attack?
Pullen (*without thinking*) Sir Justin.
Marami You?
Pullen Yes! No!

Act I

Sir Frederick No!
Pullen (*hastily realizing*) No, sir. Just in that room he attacked er, er ...
Sir Frederick Pullen.
Pullen Yes? I mean yes, Pullen.
Marami And who is this Pullen?
Pullen The accountant.
Marami Why should he go for the accountant in the bedroom?
Pullen Well, you can't do it out here, can you, you might bump into someone.
Marami Oh, Pullen's "like that" as well, is he?
Pullen Oh yes, he's like that!

Marami looks away. Sir Frederick gives a "camp" flap of his hand. Pullen flaps his hand

I mean, we're all like that!
Marami But why did your friend Stokes-Adams attack the accountant in the bedroom?
Pullen Well, we were all in there together and it got out of hand.
Sir Frederick Yes, well, I don't think His Highness wants to go into the intimate details of your private affairs, Holbrook.
Marami No, only in so far as it affects the running of this company. And it's quite obvious that this accountant is a dangerous man to have around.
Pullen Why?
Marami He could resort to blackmailing you over your relationship with Stokes-Adams.
Pullen (*forgetting his present identity*) I wouldn't—I wouldn't say that.
Marami Nevertheless, you must fire him.
Pullen I can't.
Marami You must. I insist.
Pullen Sir Frederick, I appeal to you!
Sir Frederick (*sternly*) Do as he says, Holbrook.
Pullen (*meekly*) Very well (*He goes to the desk and writes on the pad.*) "Pullen must go." I'll tell him on Monday.
Marami No, remove the bad fruit before the rot spreads. Go in and fire him now.
Pullen Now?
Marami At once.
Sir Frederick Do as he says, Holbrook!

Pullen moves to the bedroom, and half-way there remembers to assume a "camp" walk. He exits

Marami I'm glad I heard about this in time. I thank Allah that my own appetites lie in a different direction.
Sir Frederick Young, nubile maidens, eh?
Marami No, not any more. I prefer more domestic comforts.
Sir Frederick You surprise me.
Marami I've had so many wives and concubines. And the diet is frankly too rich. I yearn for the simple fare. A nice, cosy, suburban Englishwoman would be very nice.

Sir Frederick I'm inclined to agree.

Valerie enters from the bedroom

Sir Frederick and Marami rise

Valerie (*to Sir Frederick*) What on earth's the matter with Pullen ... (*She sees Marami*) Oh, I'm sorry.

Sir Frederick My dear, His Highness Sheik Marami, this is Lady Holbrook.

Valerie moves to Marami

Valerie How do you do, Your Highness?

Marami Delighted to meet you. I'm very sorry about Pullen, but it was the only course in the circumstances.

Valerie I couldn't make head or tail of what he was talking about.

Marami Your husband's had to fire him.

Valerie My husband? But he's flat on his back with Stokes-Adams.

Marami Exactly, and Pullen didn't like it. He was jealous of your husband.

Sir Frederick goes to the bedroom door and shuts it

Valerie Jealous of my husband having Stokes-Adams?

Marami Yes.

Valerie You mean he wants it too?

Marami It may seem strange, but he does.

Sir Frederick (*ushering her on to the balcony*) I'm sure you'd like some fresh air after being in that stuffy room. Come on to the balcony for a moment. Will you excuse us, Your Highness?

Marami By all means.

Valerie (*to Marami*) Please make yourself comfortable. Treat this as your own home. (*She moves to the balcony*)

Marami It is.

Valerie (*turning back, puzzled*) What?

Sir Frederick (*as they go*) I'll try and explain, my dear.

Valerie and Sir Frederick exit along the balcony. Marami sits in the chair behind the desk

Mrs Pullen knocks on the main doors. Marami ignores it. She knocks again and enters tentatively. She is a pretty, suburban lady and is carrying a small suitcase

Mrs Pullen Arthur ... Arthur, it's me ...

Marami Yes?

Mrs Pullen (*taken aback*) Oh, pardon me, I think I must be in the wrong office.

Marami (*looking over her favourably*) Which office do you want?

Mrs Pullen Holbrook's, my husband works here, in accounts, he came in early to finish off some work before going on holiday.

Marami (*beginning to ogle her*) Yes? Yes?

Mrs Pullen (*a trifle alarmed*) Yes, and I thought I might leave this case with him. I'm going to do a bit of last-minute shopping and it's rather heavy.

Marami Please allow me (*He takes the case and puts it below the office door. Mrs Pullen moves into the room. Marami follows her*)

Act I 23

Mrs Pullen Oh, I don't whether I should. I mean, I don't know you, do I?
Marami Allow me to introduce myself. Marami.
Mrs Pullen Pleased to meet you, do you work here?
Marami I'm planning to.
Mrs Pullen Oh. Yes, my husband said they were thinking of taking on foreign people. Well, good luck to you. They do say that London Airport and British Railways would grind to a halt if it wasn't for our friends from the Commonwealth. Frankly, I think it adds a bit of colour—oh, no offence meant, of course.
Marami Of course not.

Mrs Pullen sits on the sofa

Mrs Pullen And what is your line of work?
Marami I deal in money.
Mrs Pullen Oh, accounting and all that. I expect you'll be working under my husband, Mr Pullen.
Marami Pullen? Oh, so you are the poor unfortunate Mrs Pullen.
Mrs Pullen Unfortunate?
Marami It must be a wretched life for you being married to a man like that.
Mrs Pullen Well, he has his funny ways, I know, but he's not that bad.
Marami You are a very tolerant woman.
Mrs Pullen You have to be. Marriage is give and take, isn't it?
Marami And you don't object to his male friends?
Mrs Pullen Well, he hasn't got many, only his colleagues in the Coulsdon Sea Scouts.
Marami Ah, he is a Navy man; that accounts for it.
Mrs Pullen Accounts for what?
Marami Then you don't know about him and Sir Justin. (*He sits on the sofa*)
Mrs Pullen (*visibly shaken*) No. Of course I've met Sir Justin at office functions, he seemed a very nice man.
Marami Exactly. So is Mr Stokes-Adams.
Mrs Pullen I've never heard of him.
Marami Your husband came between them.
Mrs Pullen Came between them? How?
Marami In the bedroom.
Mrs Pullen My husband was in the bedroom with Sir Justin and a Mr Adams?
Marami He found them in bed together.
Mrs Pullen Oh my Lord.
Marami He was very upset.
Mrs Pullen Well, he would be, he doesn't like that sort of thing.
Marami He attacked Stokes-Adams.
Mrs Pullen Oh, he shouldn't have done that.
Marami I'm sorry to say his jealousy got the better of him.
Mrs Pullen Jealousy?
Marami He wanted to keep Sir Justin to himself.
Mrs Pullen Whatever for?
Marami Surely you know he's a practising homosexual.
Mrs Pullen Sir Justin?

Marami Your husband, Mrs Pullen.
Mrs Pullen *Arthur?*
Marami And that's why they had to fire him!
Mrs Pullen Fire?
Marami But don't worry, good lady. (*He takes Mrs Pullen's hand*) Tell me, did he never give you cause to wonder at him?
Mrs Pullen Well, as a matter of fact he hasn't bothered me much lately.
Marami Well, now you know why.
Mrs Pullen Do you mean to tell me that my Arthur is one of those ... I'll never be able to hold my head up in Coulsdon again.
Marami Leave Coulsdon. (*He gets his arms round her*) Leave Arthur. Come away with me. I will make you my chief woman.
Mrs Pullen Get your hands off.
Marami You're soft and warm and you have everything I want in a woman.
Mrs Pullen You're crazy.
Marami Yes, with desire, my loins yearn for you.
Mrs Pullen Don't be disgusting!

She rises and moves away. Marami follows her

Marami Let me rain kisses on you, and ravish you in my suite at Claridge's.

He takes her in his arms. Mrs Pullen almost swoons as he kisses her

Mrs Pullen Ah—h—h ...
Marami My little sweetmeat. It's been too much for you. Come, I will take you into the fresh morning air.

Marami bears Mrs Pullen on to the balcony and puts her on the garden seat

> *Pullen enters from the bedroom with Holbrook, who is looking weak but can just about stagger. The tablets are beginning to make him comically demented. Stella also comes in, supporting him*

Holbrook What on earth do you mean, Stokes-Adams is my name and you're supposed to be me?
Pullen It was all Sir Frederick's idea, we've got to do it for Queen and Country.
Holbrook Stokes-Adams is a medical condition. Everyone knows that.
Pullen Not Marami. And what's more, you're a homosexual from the Foreign Office.
Stella He certainly wasn't one last night.
Holbrook Thank you. What are you babbling about, Pullen?
Pullen (*hastily*) No, no, you mustn't call me that, he's gone.
Holbrook Gone?
Pullen He made me fire myself.
Holbrook Oh God, and I thought I was feeling better. Let me sit down.

Marami enters from the balcony and sees Pullen with with his arm round Holbrook, in what he assumes is an embrace

Marami Ah! Your friend, no doubt. I'm glad to see he is recovering from his attack.

Act I

Pullen (*switching on the camp manner*) Oh yes, he's feeling a teensy bit better. (*To Holbrook*) Aren't you, Stokesy?
Holbrook (*blankly*) Huh?
Pullen Come along, love, let's get you lying down.

Pullen, Holbrook and Stella sit on the sofa

Holbrook I don't want to go back to bed.
Pullen (*to Marami*) He's so stubborn, this one. (*To Holbrook*) Do as you're told, Stokes, or I'll smack your wrist.
Holbrook (*to Stella*) What's the matter with Pullen?
Pullen There is no Pullen; he's been fired, you silly thing. (*To Marami*) Memory like a sieve. Give him two more tablets, Nurse.

Stella goes to the desk and gets the tablets

Stella Can't make him any worse.
Marami Ah, you're a nurse.
Pullen Yes. You're a nurse, aren't you?
Stella At the moment. But I'm hoping to get out of it.
Marami You must not say that. It is a most noble calling. One of the oldest professions.
Stella Not quite the oldest.
Marami I wonder if you could do a little favour for me on the balcony.
Stella In broad daylight? Not likely.

Stella sits on the sofa

Marami I have a woman lying down out there and she needs your attention.
Pullen What woman?
Marami Mrs Pullen.
Pullen (*alarmed*) Mrs Pull ... (*He darts on to the balcony, has a quick look and darts back again*) Good God! What's happened to her?
Marami She's had rather a shock, that's all. I had to tell her about her husband.
Pullen And what precisely did you tell her?
Marami The plain facts, Sir Justin, that he attacked your boyfriend here, and accordingly had to be fired.
Pullen Yes, I can see that might've upset her.
Marami That wasn't what made her faint. It was when I told her I was going to take her away to be my chief woman.
Pullen (*with righteous indignation*) How dare you! (*He slaps Marami's wrist, then quickly back-pedals*) I mean—how dare you! I happen to know she wouldn't like it.
Marami I shall convert her to my tastes. It will be an interesting challenge.
Holbrook (*still semi-conscious*) Am I seeing things, or is there an Arab in my room?
Pullen Not your room, mine—you silly thing.
Holbrook Where am I then?

Pullen sits on the sofa

Pullen Never mind where you are, you don't even seem to know who you are.
Holbrook I'm still feeling peculiar.
Pullen That's why we sent for the doctor.
Holbrook I don't want an Arab doctor.
Pullen That's Marami.
Holbrook I don't want your army doctor either.

Sir Frederick and Valerie enter from the balcony

Valerie (*to Sir Frederick as she enters*) Yes, I think I understand, but who's that woman out there? She looks vaguely familiar.
Sir Frederick No idea.
Holbrook (*recognizing the voice*) Isn't that my wife?
Pullen You haven't got a wife, you daft thing, only me.
Holbrook (*straining to make some sense of it*) She looks like Valerie.
Sir Frederick Quite right, she is.
Marami And she's married to your boyfriend here.
Holbrook But I didn't get divorced, did I?
Sir Frederick No, it was annulment.
Pullen Non-consummation.
Holbrook Good Lord.
Mrs Pullen (*knocking on the window*) Somebody help me, I don't feel at all well.
Pullen (*starting to go to the balcony*) It's all right, my dear, don't ... (*Abruptly, to Stella*) Don't just sit there, Nurse, do something.
Stella What?
Marami Get a glass of water.

Stella goes to the drinks cabinet and pours a glass of water

Mrs Pullen (*on the balcony*) Arthur, was that my Arthur?
Sir Frederick Do be quiet, Madam.
Marami I will go to her.
Sir Frederick No, Your Highness, please, leave her to us. (*He hurries on to the balcony*)
Valerie You might upset her again. Come along, Nurse, and bring a glass of water. (*She hastens on to the balcony*)
Holbrook Ah, water. (*He grabs it from her and drinks it down*) That's better, things are beginning to get a little clearer in my mind.
Pullen Don't be so naughty. Give that glass back to Nurse.

Stella takes the glass and goes on to the balcony

Holbrook You can't speak to me like that.
Pullen (*petulantly*) Don't you use that tone of voice to me, Stokesy, or I might go off you. (*He goes to Holbrook and holds him. There is a struggle*) Go back to bed and wait for the doctor.

Holbrook frees himself from Pullen

Act I

Holbrook I seem to remember there was going to be some sort of catastrophe, and then the attack came.

Marami goes to Holbrook

Marami That was the accountant.
Holbrook (*to Pullen*) But aren't you one of those?
Pullen Of course, sweety, we both are.
Holbrook (*still very puzzled*) What are you talking like that for?
Pullen Because I'm livid! You're showing me up in front of the Sheik.
Holbrook I don't understand, Pullen.
Pullen I don't understand him either, jealous little minx.
Marami I hope he won't give you any more trouble, Sir Justin.
Pullen No, he won't.
Holbrook (*to Pullen, angrily*) Why don't you let me speak for myself.
Pullen Because you're *not* yourself, not at the moment, are you, "treasure"? Come on, get your clothes on. We don't want everyone talking about us! (*He pulls Holbrook*)
Marami No wonder your country is in such dire straits!
Holbrook Get your hands off me, you're molesting me!
Pullen Enough of your tantrums! I'm only trying to help! Come on, lover boy, let's get back to the bedroom.

Pullen and Holbrook struggle again and fall on the sofa. Mrs Pullen comes in from the balcony and moves to the sofa. Sir Frederick, Stella and Valerie follow her

Mrs Pullen Arthur, Arthur.
Pullen (*shouting at her*) Get out, woman, you'll ruin everything.
Mrs Pullen Arthur!
Pullen Go away woman! Can't you see we're engaged.

Mrs Pullen faints in Marami's arms, as—

the C<small>URTAIN</small> *falls*

ACT II

The same. A few moments later

Marami, Stella and Sir Frederick are trying to revive Mrs Pullen

Marami Come, we must get this lady to a chair.

Marami takes Mrs Pullen to the armchair. She sits

Sir Frederick Come along, pull yourself together, Mrs Pullen!
Marami Don't all crowd round. The poor lady needs air. And mouth-to-mouth resuscitation, Nurse.
Stella (*blankly*) And what?
Sir Frederick The kiss of life.
Stella Be my guest, she's not getting it from me.
Sir Frederick Well, somebody ought to breathe into the bag.
Marami (*angrily*) What did you say?
Sir Frederick (*hastily*) No, no, stupid of me, I was confusing it with the breathalyzer.
Marami That is for drunken drivers. Stand aside. I will breathe life into her.

Marami takes Mrs Pullen in his arms and is about to kiss her as she revives

Mrs Pullen (*half-conscious*) What are you trying to do to me?
Marami I have to kiss you.
Mrs Pullen (*trying to get up*) What?
Sir Frederick Don't distress yourself, Mrs Pullen, it's only for medical reasons.
Marami (*smiling*) Well, for the moment, yes.
Stella Excuse me, I think you've got to squeeze the nose and pull the tongue out.
Marami So be it. (*He squeezes Mrs Pullen's nose*)
Mrs Pullen (*adenoidally*) This man is mad. He's trying to squeeze my nose now, he's always trying to squeeze something.
Marami Now for that luscious little tongue. (*He starts to put his finger in her mouth*)

Mrs Pullen bites him

Ahh!!
Sir Frederick Madam, please, you've bitten the Sheik's hand.
Mrs Pullen I'll do it again if he tries it any more.
Sir Frederick But, madam, you're biting the hand that's going to feed us.
Marami Don't worry, Sir Frederick, I like it. Not only is her figure ample, but her spirit as well.

Act II

Marami embraces her again. Mrs Pullen rises and moves away from him

Mrs Pullen Get this maniac off me!

Sir Frederick Please, dear lady, let him have his way with you, it's for the good of the country.

Marami I don't need you to persuade her. I know how to handle my women.

Mrs Pullen I'm not yours and I won't be handled.

Sir Frederick Don't be difficult, Mrs Pullen.

Mrs Pullen Oh my God, you're a white-slaver! You're living off immoral earnings.

Sir Frederick Indeed I'm not. I'm a Church Commissioner.

Mrs Pullen That's even worse.

Marami And now oblige me, please, by leaving the room. We want to be alone.

Mrs Pullen I want my husband.

Stella I should forget him, dear. I wish I had your luck.

Mrs Pullen I'm not well, I want a doctor.

The telephone rings

Sir Frederick Ah, that might be him now. (*He lifts the receiver*) ... Yes, Doctor ... Oh dear ...

Mrs Pullen What's the matter?

Sir Frederick He's had a breakdown.

Mrs Pullen I know how he feels.

Sir Frederick He's trying to get through to the A.A.

Mrs Pullen I don't want him if he's on the bottle.

Marami Go and make your phone calls in another room.

Sir Frederick lays the receiver down on the desk

Sir Frederick (*ushering Stella out*) There's an extension in the office.

Marami Now you and I can get to know each other.

Mrs Pullen Don't leave me!

Sir Frederick Please, madam, it's your duty.

Mrs Pullen I don't like him, I'm frightened.

Stella (*as she goes*) Just shut your eyes.

Stella exits

Sir Frederick (*in the doorway*) And think of England.

Sir Frederick exits

Marami Now, my little desert rose, melt in my arms.

Mrs Pullen I feel hot all over.

Marami That is because I'm on fire for you. We will take my plane and fly out of the country today. At dawn we shall stand on the balcony of my palace and watch the sun rising over the desert.

Mrs Pullen I can't. We've already booked for Bournemouth.

Marami (*with contempt*) Forget Bournemouth.

Mrs Pullen We'd lose our deposit at the hotel.

Marami I will buy it for you, then.
Mrs Pullen (*amazed*) The hotel?
Marami No, Bournemouth.
Mrs Pullen Now I know you're mad.
Marami There is nothing I won't do for the woman I love if she yields to my desires. (*He embraces her*)
Mrs Pullen You keep your yields and your desires to yourself.
Marami Now give me a tempting sight of that alabaster skin.
Mrs Pullen No!

Pullen enters. He does not see Mrs Pullen at first as she is obscured by Marami

Pullen It's time to get down to things. Your Highness.
Marami (*chuckling*) I couldn't agree with you more.
Pullen (*suddenly seeing his wife*) What are you doing with my—my—my goodness me. What are you doing?
Marami Recruiting.
Pullen (*desperately trying to save his wife without giving the game away*) You mustn't do that here.
Marami Very well then, clear the bedroom.
Pullen You mustn't do it there either. You can't do it anywhere. Not with her. I won't permit it.
Marami Why do I have to have your permission?
Pullen She's a respectable married woman.
Mrs Pullen That's right, you tell him.
Pullen I've told him.
Mrs Pullen Well, tell him again. Tell him who I'm married to.
Pullen I'll tell you to whom she's married to too.
Mrs Pullen Oh for pity's sake, before he has his way with me, tell him, Arthur.
Pullen (*quickly*) Arthur! That's it! (*He sits on the sofa*) You're married to Arthur. (*To Marami*) She's married to Arthur.
Marami And you fired him in the bedroom.
Pullen I did and I didn't.
Marami Which?
Pullen I did fire him, but I didn't actually see him go off. (*He gives her mad winks*)
Mrs Pullen You've gone as mad as the others.

Sir Frederick enters and goes to the desk

Sir Frederick Just replacing the phone, the nurse can't hear.
Mrs Pullen Have you been drugging my husband?
Sir Frederick What?
Pullen Of course we haven't. (*Winking at her*) There's nothing to worry about.

Sir Frederick sits in the armchair

Sir Frederick No, nothing at all, Mrs Pullen.
Pullen (*winking*) No, nothing, Mrs Pullen.
Mrs Pullen He keeps twitching and doesn't know who he is.

Act II

Pullen What a good idea. If you'd care to step outside, madam, I'll tell you who I am. (*He winks*)
Mrs Pullen (*bursting into tears*) He's off again!
Marami The lady does not leave the room. She's mine! (*To Mrs Pullen*) You're mine!
Sir Frederick She's his.
Pullen You're his.
Mrs Pullen But I don't want to be.
Pullen If he says you're his, you're his. (*He winks*)
Mrs Pullen You mean you're giving me away?
Sir Frederick He doesn't need you.
Marami No, he's got enough on his platter with Lady Holbrook and his boyfriend, Stokes-Adams.
Pullen Absolutely.
Mrs Pullen All these years and I never knew.
Pullen (*winking*) Well, you know now.
Marami Have you had relations with Mrs Pullen?
Pullen What!
Sir Frederick Certainly not. He's got a perfectly good wife and boyfriend of his own.
Mrs Pullen (*distraught*) What about our marriage?
Marami Marriage?
Sir Frederick A complete misunderstanding on her part. Isn't it?
Pullen Yes, she got a little tiddly at an office party once and proposed to me. It was leap year.
Mrs Pullen (*to Marami*) You've got to believe me, Arthur and I have been married for twenty-five years.
Pullen She's quite right, they have.
Mrs Pullen (*to Marami*) What does he mean, "they"? Arthur and him are exactly the same.
Sir Frederick Yes, we know they are. But we try not to talk about it, madam.
Marami Now let me explain to you, my dear. You see they are all birds of a feather, and your husband is the cuckoo in the nest. You must accept it. (*To Pullen*) You can't help yourselves, can you, my dear fellow?
Pullen (*camping and winking*) No, some are born with it and some achieve it and some have it thrust upon them.

Pullen now mimes to Mrs Pullen that he is not really "gay". Marami is kissing Mrs Pullen's hand and does not see this

Mrs Pullen My husband's not well, he's sick.
Marami I'll send your husband to hospital before we go.
Mrs Pullen Go? No, I'm not going to leave my Arthur.
Pullen Touching, very touching, isn't it, Sir Frederick?
Sir Frederick Damn nuisance.
Marami If your husband's well-being means so much to you Mrs Pullen, then I will send for him when he comes out of hospital and make him one of my servants.
Sir Frederick Good idea. He'd make a splendid eunuch.

Mrs Pullen (*appalled*) Eunuch! Ahh!! (*She goes into a dead faint into Marami's arms*)

Marami She's fainted.

Pullen Just as well.

Marami You have upset her, you unfeeling goats. Come—(*He lifts her up*)—my precious jewel, I will take you back to the balcony. (*He does so*) Kindly inform me when Rubinstein arrives.

Sir Frederick Of course.

Marami and Mrs Pullen exit to the balcony and go off

Pullen Don't take her too near the edge, she has a very bad head for heights.

Sir Frederick Sh! Sh!

Pullen (*to Marami*) Or so I'm told. (*Quietly*) If I'd known my dear wife was going to be involved in all this I would never have agreed.

Sir Frederick She's turning out to be quite a useful asset.

Pullen As long as he doesn't go in for asset stripping.

Sir Frederick You'll just have to turn a blind eye.

Pullen But he's threatened to take her away.

Sir Frederick (*diplomatically*) Of course, if a knighthood isn't enough, how would you feel about a life peerage?

Pullen (*impressed*) A peerage?

Sir Frederick (*temptingly*) "Lord Pullen."

Pullen (*savouring it*) Lord Pullen of Coulsdon. I like it, I like it

Valerie enters from the bedroom

Valerie Where's the doctor? I'm sure Justin's getting worse.

Sir Frederick Is he still unconscious?

Valerie No, he's conscious, but he's talking gibberish.

Sir Frederick The doctor's car's broken down, but he's recommended someone else. The nurse is phoning him now. I'll go and see what's happening. Nurse! Nurse!

Sir Frederick exits to the office

Valerie Poor Justin! His mind is wandering! It must be the tablets he's been taking all day. He thinks he's at Kennedy Airport!

Pullen Where?

Valerie Kennedy Airport.

There is a knock at the door

The doctor at last. (*She opens the main doors*)

Pullen steps to kitchen door

Rubinstein enters with briefcase and hat. He is a smartly dressed lawyer

Thank goodness you've arrived. (*She takes his hat and puts it on the record player*)

Rubinstein I'm sorry if I've kept you waiting. I hope you haven't run out of patience.

Act II

Valerie No, hurry, he's in here. (*She pushes him towards the bedroom*) You've come across Stokes-Adams before, have you?

Rubinstein stops and looks at Pullen

Rubinstein Stokes-Adams? No, I've never had the pleasure (*He shakes Pullen warmly by the hand*) How do you do? How are you?
Pullen (*thoroughly confused*) I beg your pardon?
Rubenstein I said, how are you?
Valerie Hurry up, he's not at all well.
Rubinstein (*to Pullen*) I'm sorry to hear that, you should have a check-up.
Valerie Not him. It's my husband. He's in the bedroom, and he's having delusions. (*She opens the bedroom door*)
Rubinstein Oh, then we'd better not delay the execution.
Valerie Heavens, he's not that bad!

Rubinstein exits to the bedroom

Valerie shuts the bedroom door

Would you ask the nurse to come in as well, please.
Pullen Nurse? What nurse?
Valerie Your wife.
Pullen Wife? What wife?
Valerie Your second wife.
Pullen Oh, that one, yes, I'd forgotten for the moment. I'm so concerned about the first one.
Valerie Where is she?
Pullen The first one or the second one?
Valerie The second one.
Pullen Ah, that one's in the office, but my first one is flat out on the balcony with the Sheik. And I'm most unhappy about it.
Valerie How nice of you to be concerned.
Pullen Well, she's a very sensitive lady and that Sheik is treating her like a harlot.
Valerie You still feel protective towards her?
Pullen Of course.
Valerie You must have parted on very good terms.
Pullen We did, yes.
Valerie You must be a very sincere man.
Pullen I am, I am.
Valerie (*genuinely*) Quite a change for me to be married to a nice man. I'm rather sorry it's only temporary.
Pullen (*slightly embarrassed*) Lady Holbrook, please.
Valerie You must get used to calling me Valerie.
Pullen Ah—yes—well—I must remember that.
Valerie (*taking his arm*) I think if you let yourself go you could be quite a ladies' man.
Pullen Really?

Valerie (*slipping her arms round his neck*) If ever you should feel like making our arrangement a little more permanent, let me know.

Pullen, getting hot under the collar, casts an anxious glance to the balcony

Pullen Yes—I—er—I will.
Valerie Meanwhile, have this as a little reminder.

She gives him a kiss on the cheek, which reduces him to a jelly

Pullen Please, Lady Hol—Hol—Hol—Holy mackerel!

Stella enters

Stella I managed to get through.
Valerie (*startled*) Oh.
Pullen (*equally startled*) Ah, it's—my wife.
Valerie It isn't what you think, Mrs Pullen.
Stella (*blankly*) What isn't?
Valerie There's nothing between me and your husband.
Stella Isn't there?
Pullen She's a bit annoyed, I can tell, she won't show it now, but she'll give me hell later. Won't you, dear?
Stella (*the penny dropping*) Yes, I will. (*She pretends to be angry*) I've a good mind not to go to Bournemouth with you.
Valerie There's no need to get so upset. Your husband—my temporary and acting one—we're just trying to behave like a normally married couple in case Marami and that lady out there were looking at us.
Pullen (*spinning round*) She wasn't, was she?

Pullen moves up, looks at the bench on the balcony, and returns

Valerie I don't want to be the cause of any domestic quarrel between you.
Stella All right, but don't make a habit of it, will you, Alfred.
Valerie Alfred?
Pullen Arthur! (*He explains to Valerie*) It's Alfred Arthur.
Valerie "A.A." My goodness, fancy your parents foisting those initials on to you.
Pullen Yes, well, I was named after my father. He was a drunken patrolman.
Valerie How very sad for your mother.
Pullen Yes, poor soul, he ran her over.
Valerie Really? When?
Pullen Whenever he could.
Valerie Well, hurry up and kiss your wife. I want her to go to the doctor.
Pullen What for? What's wrong with her?
Valerie Nothing's wrong with her. I want her to go to the doctor who's in there with my husband.
Stella The doctor?
Valerie Yes.
Stella He can't be! I've only just finished speaking to him on the phone.

All three look at the office door

Act II

Valerie Then who on earth was that?

All three look at the bedroom door

> *Rubinstein comes shooting out of the bedroom, holding some torn sheets of a document. He looks somewhat ruffled. He moves to Valerie*

Rubinstein What have I done to deserve this?
Valerie How dare you go in there disturbing that poor man!
Rubinstein I wish I hadn't.
Pullen It's outrageous, pretending to be a doctor.
Rubinstein Doctor? Did I say I was a doctor?
Pullen You must've done. I expect it slipped out in the course of conversation.
Rubinstein Conversation, he says. When did I have any conversation? I hardly had time to say a polite "how do you do" before I'm whisked into the bedroom and find myself confronted by a madman who goes for me with no clothes on.
Valerie What have you done to him? Nurse, quickly!

Valerie dashes into the bedroom, followed by Stella

Rubinstein Please, please. Would you mind telling me what's going on here? I find myself in a bedroom with a man who I take it is Sir Justin Holbrook. I wake him up, show him the documents and does he read them? No, he tears them in my face. I bend down to pick them up, and he kicks me on the posterior and says I'm trying to ruin him. I turn round and ask him very politely for an explanation and all he says is "wake me up when we get to Heathrow". How can you do business with this kind of a man?
Pullen Would you by any chance be Mr Rubinstein?
Rubinstein Would I by any chance be Mr Rubinstein? Of course I'm Mr Rubinstein, everybody knows I'm Mr Rubinstein.
Pullen We didn't.
Rubinstein That's painfully obvious.
Pullen I'm afraid there's been a misunderstanding. That man in there is very sick.
Rubinstein You don't have to tell me he's sick, he should be certified. How can I tell my client that Sir Justin Holbrook didn't sign the documents, he tore them up instead?
Pullen Ah, that's my point. Sir Justin didn't tear them up.
Rubinstein So what are all these bits in my hand for? Am I going on a paper chase?
Pullen No, you don't understand, that man in there is Stokes-Adams.
Rubinstein But the lady said you were Stokes-Adams, she introduced us.
Pullen No, I'm afraid you got the wrong end of the stick. I'm Sir Justin.
Rubinstein Then why didn't you say so before?
Pullen Because we thought you were our doctor.
Rubinstein Don't you know your doctor?
Pullen Yes, but he's sending another one because he's had a breakdown.
Rubinstein That doesn't surprise me if he's got many patients like that one. (*Holding out the documents*) Look what he's done. I've got to start all

over again. Now I shall have to go all the way back to Cricklewood! I've got no staff, no heating ...
Pullen Well, you can use my—my accountant's office in there.
Rubinstein Much obliged. Thank heavens the Sheik hasn't arrived yet.
Pullen He has.
Rubinstein What?
Pullen He's out there on the balcony.

Rubinstein goes and looks at the balcony, then moves back to Pullen

Rubinstein Oh my Lord, I'd better be quick. Don't tell him what's happened and don't tell him I'm here. I knew I'd be punished, working on a Saturday.

Rubinstein exits to the office

Pullen starts to go to the balcony

Holbrook enters with Valerie and Stella from the bedroom. He is very disorientated, and although he is still in pyjamas and dressing-gown, is carrying an airways shoulder bag

Holbrook You can never hear those damned announcements!
Valerie You ought to be in bed still.
Holbrook Stop fussing. Take me to the V.I.P. Lounge, I've got to get the next flight to London.

Holbrook sits on the stool. Valerie and Stella stand either side of him

Stella You're in London.
Holbrook You're all conspiring against me.
Pullen We're just trying to save the country.
Holbrook You mind your own business, Steward, and bring me a dry Martini.
Valerie Lie down and wait for the doctor.
Holbrook No.
Valerie Do as you're told.
Holbrook You can't talk to me like that, young woman, you sound just like my wife.
Stella He still doesn't know where he is.
Holbrook I must keep awake. I have these awful nightmares. I see myself in London with all these people in my office trying to ruin me.
Pullen You're quite wrong, sir.
Holbrook And that accountant fellow, Pullen, he's at the bottom of it.
Pullen No, sir.
Holbrook Then there's this man in a shroud and a lunatic lawyer who wants me to sign myself away. Have they announced my flight yet, Steward?
Pullen (*not quite knowing what to say*) I—I—really don't know, sir.
Holbrook You're useless, just like that man Pullen.
Valerie (*humouring Holbrook*) We'll let you know when it's called.

Marami enters from the balcony

Marami Has Rubinstein arrived yet, Holbrook?

Act II

Pullen (*whispering*) No, he hasn't.
Holbrook Who's addressing me?
Pullen No-one.
Holbrook Someone said Holbrook.
Marami It was me, Mr Adams. I was talking to your friend.
Pullen (*remembering his "role"*) Oh, yes. That's right.
Holbrook What?
Pullen You be quiet. It's nothing to do with you. (*To Marami*) He's on the wander again.
Holbrook You're all trying to keep me here. You don't want me to board that plane.
Valerie Nonsense, you'll be the first on board when it's called.
Holbrook And where's that damn Martini?
Pullen Right away, sir!
Marami (*to Pullen*) You are right, your poor friend is wandering.
Pullen Oh, I know, in an awful pickle, that one. Doesn't know if he's coming or going.

Marami moves close to Holbrook

Marami Yes, a very sad case.
Holbrook (*turning and becoming aware of Marami*) Ah! It's you again. You're after me, aren't you?

Marami moves. Pullen moves to Holbrook

Pullen No, love, no.
Holbrook And that mad solicitor, Rubinstein.
Marami What? Rubinstein here? My solicitor?
Pullen (*quickly*) No, he said his mad sister. He was talking about his mad sister, Ruby—Ruby Stein, she married a hairdresser in Wimbledon. (*To Holbrook*) Never got over it, did you, love?
Holbrook (*bemused*) Not really, no.

Sir Frederick enters from the office

Sir Frederick What's all this about him tearing up important documents?
Marami What important documents, Sir Frederick?
Sir Frederick Oh, nothing to worry about, Your Highness.
Marami You said important documents.
Holbrook Ah! Documents!
Marami They're here?
Pullen No, not your documents. His documents, for travel, he tore up his passport.
Holbrook I've got my passport in there. (*He points to the bedroom*)
Pullen Oh good, then you can board, love.
Holbrook Ah! Security check?

Holbrook raises his arms and Pullen frisks him

Pullen She loves these little games, you know. Take him to the plane, girls, and give him a nice window seat.
Valerie Come along.
Holbrook This is a lousy airport. I never got that drink.

Holbrook, Stella and Valerie exit to the bedroom

Sir Frederick Would somebody kindly explain how we got on to airports?
Pullen He thinks he's at Kennedy Airport.
Sir Frederick Oh God. (*He sits in the armchair*)

Mrs Pullen comes in from the balcony

Mrs Pullen I'm feeling a little better now, and I want to go to Bournemouth.

Marami moves to one side of Mrs Pullen, Pullen to the other

Pullen Yes, why don't we just let the poor lady go to Bournemouth, she likes it there?

Marami takes hold of Mrs Pullen

Marami No, I'm taking her to my palace.

Pullen takes hold of Mrs Pullen

  Any man who stands in my way will be incarcerated.

Pullen pushes Mrs Pullen to Marami

Mrs Pullen You're inhuman!
Pullen Please don't speak to His Highness like that.
Marami Let me take you to my car, the chauffeur will drive you back to Claridge's.

Marami and Mrs Pullen move to the main doors

Mrs Pullen I don't want to go to Claridge's. I want to go to Marks and Spencer's.
Marami My favourite store. Very well, whatever you desire. My chauffeur will go with you to see that you do not have to pay for anything you take.
Mrs Pullen I don't want to go with him. I want to go with my Arthur.
Sir Frederick But you must understand, my good woman, that your Arthur doesn't want you.
Mrs Pullen Of course Arthur wants me. (*To Pullen*) Say you want me, Arthur.
Pullen Don't keep calling me Arthur.
Mrs Pullen Why not?
Pullen Because it isn't my name—(*he winks and camps*)—you stupid thing.
Mrs Pullen What's come over you, Arthur?
Sir Frederick He's not Arthur.
Mrs Pullen Well, for pity's sake who is he then?

Mrs Pullen goes to Sir Frederick

Marami Sir Justin Holbrook.
Mrs Pullen I'm not married to Sir Justin Holbrook.

Act II

Sir Frederick Course not. You're married to Mr Pullen.
Mrs Pullen But I'm Mrs Pullen.
Pullen Nobody's said you weren't.
Sir Frederick It was you who said that Sir Justin Holbrook—(*he points to Pullen*)—was Mr Pullen. You mustn't go round saying things like that, you could get into serious trouble.
Pullen You'll be saying that you're my wife next.
Mrs Pullen I am your wife.
Pullen (*to the others*) I told you. She thinks she's Lady Holbrook now.
Mrs Pullen I don't think anything of the sort. How could I be Lady Holbrook?
Sir Frederick You can't be, he's married already.
Marami And anyway he prefers men.
Mrs Pullen What are you talking about? You're trying to confuse me.
Sir Frederick The fact is, Mrs Pullen, I'm afraid you're not very well.
Mrs Pullen Aren't I?
Pullen You've been fainting rather a lot lately.
Sir Frederick Probably just a little disturbance of the brain.
Marami You have nothing to fear, when you're living in my palace you will have the very latest treatment from my psychiatrist.
Mrs Pullen (*holding on to Pullen*) I don't want a psychiatrist and a palace, I want my husband in Bournemouth.
Sir Frederick We'll do our best to trace him for you.
Mrs Pullen Trace him?
Sir Frederick Yes we'll put an advertisement in *Gay News*.
Mrs Pullen You're wicked, all of you.
Marami Calm yourself. (*He goes to her and puts his arm round her*)
Mrs Pullen Don't you touch me, you desert gigolo.
Pullen (*restraining her*) Be quiet, madam.
Mrs Pullen (*shouting*) I won't! I won't! I'm being attacked by maniacs. (*She rushes on to the balcony shouting*) Help! Police!

They rush after her

If you touch me I'll jump! Taxi! Taxi!

They get hold of her and drag her back, struggling

Marami How strong she is, magnificent.
Mrs Pullen Let me go!
Sir Frederick We'll have to sedate her.
Pullen The doctor's coming, my dear. He'll give you something.
Sir Frederick She'll have to be put away somewhere.

Mrs Pullen starts to have hysterics

She's having hysterics, slap her face.

Pullen Who? Me? I couldn't.
Sir Frederick Well, I will.
Marami No. There is a much gentler way.
Pullen How? Cold water?
Marami No, cold steel.

Sir Frederick What?
Marami You simply show the patient a knife.
Pullen (*holding his wife protectively*) Good heavens!
Marami Quickly, we must find one.
Sir Frederick There must be one in the kitchen.
Marami (*looking round*) Kitchen?
Sir Frederick (*pointing to the kitchen*) In there, Your Highness.
Marami Ah.

Marami exits to the kitchen

Sir Frederick Stop it, woman. (*To Pullen*) Explain to your wife.
Pullen (*sitting his wife down on the sofa*) Joyce, listen. We're not doing what you think we are, I'm still your Arthur, but I'm also Sir Justin married to Lady Holbrook and to Stella and to you because Holbrook's in bed with Stokes-Adams, so he can't sign the papers with Marami, and Sir Frederick says if I do it you can be Lady Pullen of Coulsdon. It's as simple as that.

Mrs Pullen bursts into fresh hysterics

Marami rushes back into the room with a carving knife, shows it to her and she subsides immediately

Marami You see?
Pullen Good Lord, it works.
Marami Of course, it never fails. I do it to all my women.
Pullen Why don't you use cold water?
Marami Have you ever tried finding cold water in the desert?
Pullen Shall I get her a cup of coffee?
Marami No, no, strong tea. Fortunately I have some sedatives in my car.
Sir Frederick Would you like me to fetch them?
Marami No, I will do it personally. You make the lady a cup of tea.
Sir Frederick Make tea? That's a bit thick. After all, I'm a privy councillor.
Marami (*sternly*) Do as I ask.
Sir Frederick (*meekly*) One lump or two.
Pullen (*without thinking*) Two.
Marami How do you know?
Pullen Oh, er—I don't—but I thought she looked like a lady who has two lumps—takes two lumps.
Marami Lay up a tray, Sir Frederick, and serve it properly for the lady.
Sir Frederick Very good, Your Highness.

Sir Frederick exits to the kitchen

Marami She seems a little calmer now. You better take the knife, Holbrook, whilst I get the sedatives.
Pullen If you insist.

Pullen takes the knife gingerly, and Mrs Pullen follows it with her eyes in a sort of trance

Act II

Marami It is obvious to me that this lady is suffering from years of frustration because of her unfeeling husband.
Pullen Oh, she is, yes.
Marami He must be a thoughtless brute.
Pullen Complete bounder.
Marami I can't understand why you allowed yourself to be involved with him.
Pullen It was a moment of mental aberration.

Without thinking Pullen lowers the knife. Mrs Pullen screams

Marami The knife!

Pullen puts the knife back

Pullen You see, he found out about me and my friend Stokes ...

Mrs Pullen starts to have hysterics again as Pullen lowers the Knife

Marami Quick, the knife. Keep showing her the knife.
Pullen Yes, I'm sorry.

Pullen shows her the knife and she subsides. Marami goes to the main doors

Marami I will get her the sedatives. I want her calm for later.
Pullen Later?
Marami Yes, we shall be flying home.
Pullen Oh, yes.
Marami (*with a chuckle*) You have never had a woman till you've had one in a jet.

Marami exits

Pullen (*to himself*) She even has to have her back to the engine on the train! (*To Mrs Pullen*) Are you feeling calmer now, dear? The doctor will be here soon and then you can be on your way.

The telephone rings. Pullen looks at it and makes two or three attempts to reach it, still showing Mrs Pullen the knife. Eventually he gives her the knife, goes to the telephone, brings it to the sofa, and takes the knife from her

(*On the phone*) Hello ... Dr Fosgrove said we could expect you. We're on the thirty-eighth floor.

He takes the knife away. Mrs Pullen screams. He puts the knife back

(*To Mrs Pullen*) Shut up, woman ... No, the trouble is I'm trying to control my wife with this knife; so for goodness sake hurry.

Pullen quickly puts the telephone back on the desk. Mrs Pullen screams. Pullen goes back to Mrs Pullen and bends double, showing her the knife

Rubinstein enters with the new documents

Rubinstein All this noise. How can I concentrate on my documents? ... (*sees the back view of Pullen*) My God!
Pullen (*hastily*) It's all right, I'm only showing it to her.

Rubinstein Showing it to her?
Pullen She's having hysterics.
Rubinstein I'm not surprised.
Pullen Are the papers ready for signing?
Rubinstein Yes, Sir Justin.
Mrs Pullen (*whimpering*) He's not Sir Justin.
Rubinstein I beg your pardon?
Pullen She's a bit peculiar—(*confidentially*)—in the head. (*He taps his head*) As soon as we get this signed, she'll be sent away.
Rubinstein I can recommend a very good sanatorium in Brighton. Belongs to my cousin.
Mrs Pullen Why can't I go to Bournemouth?
Rubinstein My cousin doesn't live in Bournemouth.
Mrs Pullen But we've booked Bournemouth.
Pullen She likes it there. She goes there every year.
Rubinstein Every year? What a sad case.
Pullen As soon as I've signed these papers she can be on her way.
Mrs Pullen I won't let you sign. I won't be sent away.

Mrs Pullen rises, goes to Rubinstein, takes the documents, tears them in half and drops the pieces on the floor

Rubinstein (*shocked*) My documents. You let her tear my documents.
Pullen I'm frightfully sorry.
Rubinstein Sorry, you say. What's the good of being sorry? I could kill her for this!

Mrs Pullen rushes hysterically to Pullen. He takes her in his arms

Pullen No, you must control yourself.
Rubinstein Give me that knife.
Pullen Certainly not.
Mrs Pullen Don't let him near me. Tell the horrible doctor to go away.
Rubinstein Doctor? Why does everyone think I'm a doctor? I don't look like a doctor, do I? Madam, look at me, please look at me.

She looks at him

Do I look like a doctor?

Mrs Pullen reverts to hysterics, and Pullen calms her. Rubinstein kneels and picks up the torn documents. Pullen and Mrs Pullen sit on the sofa

I'll do this once more, then I'm going to my cousin in Brighton.

Marami enters from main doors with a bottle of tablets

Marami Ah, Rubinstein, when did you get here?

Rubinstein hides the torn documents, turns upstage and bows to Marami

Rubinstein Oh, good morning, Your Highness. I've just arrived.
Marami That is impossible, I have only this minute come up in the lift myself.

Act II

Rubinstein I slipped in the back way. I mean, I don't want to be seen going into an office on a Saturday—you understand.

Marami pours a glass of water, opens the bottle of tablets and takes out two capsules

Marami (*amused*) Well done! Well done! Put the documents on the desk. We shall sign them as soon as I've given this poor lady the tablets.

Rubinstein tries to conceal the papers behind his back

Rubinstein I think I should advise you not to rush things. Let me check it first. I mean, one little mistake could cost you millions, couldn't it, Sir Justin?

Pullen forgets to answer

I'm talking to you, Sir Justin.
Pullen Oh, me, yes.
Rubinstein I was telling his Highness it could cost millions, couldn't it?
Pullen Absolutely—what could?
Rubinstein A mistake in my documents.
Marami (*to Mrs Pullen*) Take these, my dear, with a little water.

Mrs Pullen takes the glass and pills from him

Pullen They're quite safe, I hope, she's never had anything stronger than an Aspirin. (*Hastily*) So she tells me.
Marami They are a little something I had made up in the Casbah.
Rubinstein She needs knock-out drops—double strength.
Marami Let me have those documents.
Rubinstein (*handing them over reluctantly*) They're not actually what you'd call engrossed.
Pullen No more in half.
Marami What is the meaning of this, Rubinstein?
Rubinstein It's a very sad case. For some reason, which escapes me, she thinks I'm a doctor, when I don't even look like a doctor.
Pullen She thought he was threatening to send her to a loony bin in Brighton run by his cousin.
Marami Is this true?
Rubinstein Yes, it's my cousin Morris, he bought it fifteen years ago, when he sold the riding stable at Uckfield. He's been very fortunate, unlike another cousin David, poor chap, he's inside the place. I don't think he'll ever come out. But at sixty pounds a day who wants to let him go? Morris is no fool, and funnily enough he does look like a doctor ...
Marami I mean, is it true that you wanted to commit this lady to an asylum?
Pullen He was only trying to be helpful. She snatched them from him and tore them up.
Marami (*to Rubinstein*) You had no right to threaten her.
Rubinstein She had no right to tear them up. Now I've got to do them all over again.
Marami Nonsense, you fool.

Pullen If you join them together, would it be legal?
Rubinstein Legal, yes, but not very tidy. I have my firm's reputation to think of.
Pullen Frankly, speed is of the essence.

Sir Frederick enters from the kitchen with a tea tray. He puts the tray on the sofa table and sits on the sofa

Sir Frederick Sorry I've been so long. I couldn't find the instructions. I trust this will be satisfactory.
Marami I'm sure it will. Pour out a cup for the lady. My lawyer and I just want to peruse these documents. Come into the office, Rubinstein.

Rubinstein and Marami exit to the office

Pullen sits on the sofa

Pullen (*to Mrs Pullen*) Are you feeling a little calmer now?
Mrs Pullen I would be if you'd put that knife down.
Pullen All right, I will, if you promise not to scream.
Mrs Pullen I promise, but you mustn't upset me any more. (*As Pullen speaks she starts to nod off*)
Pullen Now, Joyce, listen, I'll try and tell you once more. A very delicate situation has arisen in the City, nay in the Country, due to unforeseen circumstances outside our control. In consequence of which there is a financial crisis which can only be resolved in one way. I and Sir Frederick are steering a very tricky course. Now, if all had gone well and Sir Justin had been himself I could've been myself and joined you on the five thirty to Bournemouth, full dining-car service, probably ... (*He sees that Mrs Pullen's eyes are closed and that she has nodded off*) She's gone to sleep.

Sir Frederick takes the glass from Mrs Pullen and puts it on the sofa table

Sir Frederick Wake her up!
Pullen I think she's been drugged.
Sir Frederick We all have to make sacrifices, and to give the lady her due, she's turned out to be surprisingly useful as bait.
Pullen I won't have my wife thought of as a lug-worm.
Sir Frederick There are times, Pullen, when the end justifies the means. Wake her up.

Holbrook comes in wearing a bowler hat, supported by Valerie and Stella

Holbrook That was a smooth flight. Where's my chauffeur?
Valerie Chauffeur?
Holbrook He should be here to meet me.
Stella We'll have him paged, now sit down.
Holbrook Somebody's taken my duty-frees.
Sir Frederick Nobody's taken them, you haven't got any.
Holbrook Ah. Are you my chauffeur?
Sir Frederick Certainly not.

Act II

Holbrook That's a relief. Well, when he arrives tell him I'll be out here watching the planes from the waving base.

Holbrook goes on to balcony, supported by Valerie and Stella. They sit him on the bench

Pullen A thought has just occurred to me, Sir Frederick.
Sir Frederick Yes?
Pullen If Sir Justin—er—if he shouldn't recover …
Sir Frederick Yes?
Pullen Then where would that put me?
Sir Frederick In a very serious situation.
Pullen But it's you and the Government who are forcing me to do it.
Sir Frederick Nonsense. You're doing it for personal gain, a title, remember?
Pullen But if Holbrook doesn't recover, I shall be had up for fraud.
Sir Frederick Yes, and misrepresentation.
Pullen What happens then?
Sir Frederick It'll be me and the Government prosecuting you.
Pullen (*astounded*) You wouldn't stand by me?
Sir Frederick Be fair, Pullen, we're respectable and indispensable.
Pullen You mean I'm not?
Sir Frederick Well—respectable, yes, in your own small way.
Pullen But dispensable.
Sir Frederick Don't worry, old chap, we'd give you a good character reference and look after you when you came out.
Pullen Thank you very much! (*He puts the knife on the desk*)
Sir Frederick Now I really think you'd better rouse your wife. After all, she's got to be ready to go with Marami.
Pullen How far?
Sir Frederick As far as he likes.
Pullen That's outrageous. I was prepared to overlook a little "billing and cooing", but once he signed the documents, I certainly wouldn't let him take her away!

Marami enters followed by Rubinstein, who has documents stuck together by Sellotape

Marami Everything is in order now, and I am ready to sign immediately, Holbrook.
Rubinstein Very good, this tape. One of my Scotch cousins makes it. Cousin Hymish.
Marami Then after the business is concluded I am going to bear my sleeping princess to Claridge's.
Sir Frederick Or to wherever his wishes lie, eh, Holbrook?
Pullen You've gone too far. (*To Rubinstein*) You call these documents? Give them to me.

Pullen crosses to Rubinstein, takes the documents, tears them and throws them on the floor

They're a shambles, do them again!

Rubinstein You tore my documents.
Marami Have you taken leave of your senses?
Pullen Do them again, Mr Rubinstein. And do them properly, not a quick cobbled job like that.
Rubinstein Shambles, he says. Cobbled, he called them. I'm not saying here to be insulted and have my documents torn up. (*He strides to the main doors*)
Marami Come back, Rubinstein.
Rubinstein No, I flatly refuse. You can get yourself another lawyer. On what you pay me why should I stay? (*He puts on his hat*)
Marami I'll double it.
Rubinstein I'll stay. (*He whisks his hat off and replaces it on the record player, staying by the main doors*)
Marami Good. (*He rounds on Pullen*) Now, Holbrook, explain your outrageous behaviour.
Pullen Well—er ...

There is a knock at the main doors

Ah. There's somebody at the door. I'd better answer it.
Rubinstein Please, allow me, Sir Justin. (*He opens the doors*)

A good-looking man carrying a doctor's case enters. His name is Cornish

Dr Cornish Dr Cornish.
Rubinstein Dr Cornish? No, Mr Rubinstein. Do I look like a doctor?
Dr Cornish I'm Dr Cornish.
Pullen Oh, come in.
Dr Cornish Thank you.
Pullen Fosgrove recommended you very highly.
Dr Cornish Jolly kind of him.
Pullen Tell us all about yourself.
Marami No need for that, you're wasting time.
Pullen Quite right. I mean, there's no need, I'm sure your qualifications are excellent, Dr Cornish. There's no need to check them.
Dr Cornish (*piqued*) I should hope not indeed.
Pullen Oh, nothing personal, but it's just struck me as rather odd that if someone says they're a doctor we take their word for it.
Rubinstein (*on his knees picking up the torn documents*) Yes, a very interesting point that. It could apply to lawyers—in fact it does—unless of course you're like me and look like a lawyer. That's why I can't understand why everyone thinks I look like a doctor.
Sir Frederick You don't look like a doctor to me.
Marami You don't resemble a lawyer either, with a handful of torn pages. You look more like Toulouse Lautrec. Go and put them together again at once.
Rubinstein I can't, this means a complete retype.
Marami Can you do that?
Rubinstein Yes, fortunately my cousin Phyllis has a typing school in Streatham and she taught me.
Pullen I don't believe it.

Act II

Rubinstein It's true. I've got a diploma.
Marami Rubinstein, please!
Rubinstein Sorry, I just wanted to establish my qualifications.

Rubinstein exits to the office

Dr Cornish I'm awfully sorry to interrupt all this. I think I ought to see Sir Justin right away. Where is he?
Marami (*pointing to Pullen*) Right here beside you.
Pullen What? Oh yes, so I am.
Dr Cornish Good gracious. I expected to find you lying down.
Marami He is not the patient, he is Sir Justin Holbrook.
Dr Cornish But I was told Sir Justin Holbrook was the patient.
Sir Frederick No, there must be some mistake.
Marami It is his friend.
Pullen That's right, my friend.

Holbrook comes in from the balcony with Valerie and Stella

Holbrook It's such a bore, there's nothing taking off out there, you know. (*He sees Cornish*) Are you my chauffeur?
Dr Cornish I'm Cornish.
Holbrook I don't care where you come from as long as you can drive.
Valerie He's the doctor, dear.
Dr Cornish That's right, standing in for Fosgrove. (*Looking at Pullen*) Now where is the Stokes-Adams?
Marami That's him there. (*He indicates Holbrook*)

Cornish does not see

Sir Frederick No! No! Next to Lady Holbrook.
Pullen And the nurse.
Dr Cornish You should be in bed.
Holbrook I would be if that damned chauffeur had come to take me home.
Valerie He's not completely with us, his mind is wandering.
Dr Cornish Common symptom, reduced blood supply, affects the brain. Is there somewhere I can carry out an examination?
Valerie (*pointing*) In there, Sir Justin's bedroom.
Sir Frederick He won't mind, I'm sure.
Pullen No, help yourself, please.
Holbrook That sounds like Pullen. What's he doing at the airport?
Sir Frederick Get him into bed quickly, it could be dangerous.
Dr Cornish It isn't normally, still we'd better take him through. Come along, Nurse.

Valerie and Stella usher Holbrook off to the bedroom followed by Dr Cornish

Holbrook (*as he goes*) You're not the flying doctor, are you?
Marami Now perhaps you'll tell me, Holbrook, why, without any warning or explanation, you tore up those documents.
Pullen They were totally unacceptable.

Marami You didn't even read them. You seem to forget that Sir Frederick and I drew up the heads of agreement this morning over breakfast.
Sir Frederick I don't think Sir Justin was questioning the contents (*To Pullen*) Were you?
Pullen No, I just didn't like the look of them. They were a mess.
Sir Frederick They were not worthy of Your Highness.
Pullen I didn't intend to run you into any additional expense.
Marami You haven't.
Pullen But you told Rubinstein you'd pay him double.
Marami Don't worry. I'm not going to pay him anything.
Pullen He won't like that very much.
Marami He'll like it even less if I reported him to his Rabbi for working on a Saturday.

Marami exits to the office

Mrs Pullen starts to wake up

Mrs Pullen (*waking up*) I feel hot.
Pullen Joyce? Come along, Joyce. It's me, Arthur.
Mrs Pullen Arthur?
Pullen Yes.
Mrs Pullen I've got something to tell you, Arthur.
Pullen What is it, poppet?
Mrs Pullen You're a very, very boring man.
Pullen She doesn't know what she's saying.
Mrs Pullen Oh yes, I do—boring, and I feel hot.
Sir Frederick Take her back on to the balcony.
Pullen Yes, come along, my dear. (*He starts to get her up*)

Marami appears in the office door

Mrs Pullen I don't want you ... (*She sees Marami*) I want him. (*She holds her arms out to Marami*) I want you. (*She goes towards him*)
Marami Of course you do. And I want you, my little apricot.

Mrs Pullen moves above the sofa. Marami follows

Mrs Pullen You're so strong and manly. Take me to the balcony. Don't ever send me back to that boring man in Coulsdon again.
Marami No, not in a thousand days, or nights.

Marami and Mrs Pullen embrace and then they exit to the balcony and off

Pullen She calls me boring. The stupid woman, what makes her think I'd ever want her back? I suppose she was adequate when I was just an accountant, but now that I'm in my present responsible position she would be quite useless.
Sir Frederick She's been useful to me, Pullen. We can sign the documents as soon as Rubinstein's got them ready.
Pullen Wait, Sir Frederick. When Rubinstein brings in those documents, you're expecting me to sign them.

Sir Frederick You've got to, there's no turning back now.

Pullen Then I'll do it on one condition. Now that I've become Sir Justin, I shall remain Sir Justin.

Sir Frederick What about your peerage?

Pullen Who wants to be a penniless peer when I can be a rich tycoon retired in South America.

Sir Frederick What!

Pullen That's where all the top people go to disappear, isn't it? And then you can open a numbered bank account for me in Switzerland.

Sir Frederick Where's the money coming from?

Pullen The sale of my shares to Marami.

Sir Frederick But they're not your shares.

Pullen Oh, but if I sign as Sir Justin then I own every share that belonged to him. And what's more, I get them for nothing. Those are my only terms.

Sir Frederick What happens to the real Sir Justin?

Pullen Bung him off to Australia under an assumed name, I'll give him mine if he likes, I shan't be needing it any more.

Sir Frederick What's he going to live on?

Pullen His wages, like everyone else. Do him a lot of good.

Sir Frederick But he's not qualified for anything.

Pullen I don't suppose you need any more skill to fleece sheep than you do shareholders.

Sir Frederick That's a slanderous statement.

Pullen You think so? What about the Mount Street Secretarial Agency and the rest. Very good material for a *Sunday Times* special investigation.

Sir Frederick Oh, all right, you can have the proceeds from the sale of his shares.

Pullen Thank you, sir. Just one other thing. What about the proceeds from the sale of your shares?

Sir Frederick What about them?

Pullen I don't want to run short. I'll have those as well. I expect private jets can be pretty pricy even in South America. And when things blow over I intend to do the odd spot of globe-trotting, incognito, like Howard Hughes. I fancy a drink. (*He goes to the drinks cabinet and pours a whisky*) Care to join me?

Sir Frederick No thanks, I don't like drinking with blackmailers.

Pullen (*blandly*) Oh, don't you ever drink on your own?

Sir Frederick exits to the office. Dr Cornish enters from the bedroom, goes to the desk and puts his case on it

Dr Cornish I'm not very happy about the condition of that chum of yours. I'm going to pop him round to the Clinic. They're getting him ready now.

Pullen Is he going to be all right?

Pullen sits on the sofa

Dr Cornish I would think so, but he'll need a complete break.

Pullen Don't worry, he'll get one, I'll make sure of that.

Dr Cornish He's very lucky to have a rich friend like you.

Pullen (*camping it*) Oh yes, I worry dreadfully about dear Arthur.
Dr Cornish Oh, it's Arthur, is it?
Pullen Yes, Arthur Pullen.

Dr Cornish sits on the sofa

Dr Cornish No need to worry. Diagnosis has never been Fosgrove's strong point. The fact that your chum keeps reviving and collapsing indicates to me that it isn't Stokes-Adams at all. It's an incomplete heart-block. I suspect your chum has been overdoing things.
Pullen My chum?
Dr Cornish Arthur.
Pullen Oh, he has, yes, dreadfully. I've been begging him to take things more easily for some time, but he won't.
Dr Cornish (*placing a comforting hand on Pullen*) I do understand, you know.
Pullen (*slightly alarmed*) Do you?
Dr Cornish He's very lucky to have such a faithful friend. I had one, until recently.
Pullen Oh dear, I'm awfully sorry.
Dr Cornish Oh, we went through a most beastly time. I nearly had a nervous breakdown. Still, I mustn't inflict my problems on you. I thought Kenneth and I had a very happy and successful partnership in Chelsea. You didn't know him then, I suppose.
Pullen I don't think I know him at all.
Dr Cornish 'Course you do. He's your doctor, Kenneth Fosgrove. You probably know him as Freda.
Pullen (*aghast*) No.
Dr Cornish Yes. Got too big for her boots and went off to Harley Street.
Pullen That's appalling.
Dr Cornish Didn't you know?
Pullen No.
Dr Cornish Oh dear, I hope I haven't gone too far.

Dr Cornish puts his hand on Pullen's knee

Pullen (*hastily*) Well, don't go any further.
Dr Cornish It's only when I meet someone wonderful and jolly understanding like you that I can mention it.
Pullen (*backing away*) Don't mention it.

Dr Cornish puts his arm round Pullen

Dr Cornish You must come over to dinner sometime, and bring Arthur when he's better.
Pullen I can't do that. I'm sending him away.
Dr Cornish Well, come on your jolly own, then.
Pullen Jolly kind of you, but I was thinking of going back to the wife actually.

Marami enters from the balcony

Marami Ah! Holbrook, I wondered if I could borrow your doctor.

Pullen rises and moves away

Act II

Pullen Please do. (*To Cornish*) You've no objection to looking at the lady out there, have you?
Dr Cornish No, who is she?
Pullen His lady friend.
Marami Mrs Pullen. I want to know if she will be fit to travel later today.
Dr Cornish (*to Pullen*) Your chum's got a lady wife, too?
Pullen (*madly working it out*) Yes.
Dr Cornish You really are a couple of mixed-up boys, aren't you? (*He nudges Pullen*) I can only spare a minute.

Dr Cornish picks up his case and exits to the balcony with Marami

Pullen crosses to the drinks cabinet and picks up the whisky bottle

Holbrook, Stella and Valerie enter from the bedroom. Holbrook has on a bowler hat. Stella has Holbrook's suitcase, and she collects her bag from beside the bedroom door

Holbrook Where the hell's my hand luggage?
Stella It's here.
Valerie Easy does it.
Holbrook We'll go through the Green Channel, I've got nothing to declare, only my duty-frees. (*He looks around*) Where the hell are they?
Valerie I don't know. Anyway, it doesn't matter.

Holbrook notices Pullen with the bottle of whisky

Holbrook There they are, he's got 'em.

Holbrook goes to Pullen. Pullen puts the whisky bottle on the drinks cabinet

Pullen I beg your pardon?
Holbrook Give 'em back at once.
Pullen No, they're mine now.

Holbrook takes the whisky bottle and puts it in his shoulder bag

Holbrook The devil they are.

Sir Frederick and Rubinstein enter

Sir Frederick Rubinstein's got the documents ready.
Rubinstein And a very tidy job, if I do say so myself. (*He shows them to Pullen*) Here, Sir Justin, have a look. What d'you think of that? (*He gives the documents to Pullen and then snatches them back*)
Pullen Very nice.
Rubinstein Nice? It's nothing less than a miracle, almost a custom job.
Holbrook Customs? No, I've got nothing to declare.
Rubinstein Keep that lunatic away from me.
Pullen Don't worry, he's going to the Clinic.
Rubinstein Not before time.

Dr Cornish enters from the balcony

Dr Cornish Ah, good, you've got him ready. You come with me and the nurse, Mr Pullen.
Holbrook Who's he talking to?
Rubinstein You, of course.
Holbrook Don't you call me Pullen.
Dr Cornish All right, then, Arthur.
Holbrook I'm not Arthur, either.
Rubinstein He doesn't know who he is, does he?
Pullen I'm afraid not.
Rubinstein First of all he's a Mr Adams, then he's a Mr Pullen. Now you call him Mr Arthur. He'll be saying he's Sir Frederick Goudhurst next.
Holbrook I would say a stupid thing like that. I'm Sir Justin Holbrook.
Sir Frederick Poor fellow.
Pullen Take my friend away, Doctor.

Dr Cornish, Stella and Holbrook move to the main doors

Dr Cornish Yes, this way, Arthur, come with me and the nurse.
Holbrook What about my wife?
Dr Cornish She won't bother you any more, she's quite fit enough to travel.
Holbrook I didn't know she was going anywhere.
Dr Cornish Well, that's one piece of good news for you. Come on now, and I promise you your chum can visit you whenever you like. Isn't that nice? Now off we go to the Clinic.

Stella exits through the main doors

Holbrook (*to Sir Frederick*) Hey! You! Fasten your seat belt!

Dr Cornish and Holbrook exit through the main doors. Marami enters from the balcony, and sits at the desk

Valerie sits in the armchair

Marami The documents, Rubinstein. Can we sign them now?
Rubinstein Yes, Your Highness. (*He moves to the desk*) I wish you would, and quickly, before somebody tears them up.
Sir Frederick (*moving to the desk*) Who will sign first?
Marami You and Sir Justin, please, then I will append my signature.

Sir Frederick signs the documents

Rubinstein We shall of course require two witnesses. I naturally will be one—unless of course you feel that, as I'm acting for one of the parties, I'm not sufficiently independent, in which case I can very easily get hold of Michael.
Sir Frederick Michael?
Rubinstein Yes, just round the corner, in Aldgate.
Pullen A cousin, no doubt.
Rubinstein Yes, you know him, do you? Runs a tailoring business, very well respected in the City.
Sir Frederick (*cutting in*) No, no, it's all right. We'll make do with you, Rubinstein. Come along, Holbrook, you're next.

Act II

Sir Frederick moves away from the desk. He and Pullen look at each other. Pullen moves to the desk. Sir Frederick sits on the sofa

Pullen (*taking his pen*) Where do I sign?
Rubinstein (*pointing*) Here, and here. And as for the other witness, perhaps this lady here will oblige.
Valerie I'd like to, but I'm afraid I can't, you see I'm his wife. (*She points to Pullen*) Aren't I, darling?
Pullen (*suddenly realizing his good fortune*) Yes, so you are.

Pullen goes to Valerie and takes her hand

Rubinstein Oh, so sorry, I didn't realize. If I may say so, you're a very fortunate man, Sir Justin.
Pullen Yes, I am, aren't I?
Marami I will supply the other witness—Mrs Pullen.
Pullen (*without thinking*) Ah, but she's my wi-wi—

Valerie nudges Pullen

—why not? She's my accountant's wife. You couldn't do better than her.

Marami claps his hands twice

Marami (*calling out to balcony*) Come along, Jasmine.
Pullen Jasmine?
Marami Yes, I have renamed her. I don't like Joyce.
Pullen Neither do I.

Mrs Pullen enters from the balcony, with a flower in her hair, and moves to the desk, wafting her chiffon scarf

Mrs Pullen Did you want me, Abdul?
Marami I shall always want you, but for the moment I just want your signature.
Mrs Pullen Whatever you say, dear.
Rubinstein Right, if we're all ready we can proceed.

Valeries rises and moves towards the kitchen. Pullen follows

Valerie I'll get some champagne from the kitchen, darling.
Pullen Champagne at ten thirty?
Valerie Well, we've got a lot to celebrate, haven't we?

Valerie exits to the kitchen

Pullen A whole new world.
Mrs Pullen (*ecstatically*) Yes, a whole new world. A hot passionate world where Jasmine can flower and blossom, nurtured by her lord and master, where she only has to clap her hands and they all come running. Maidens, houseboys and eunuchs.
Marami Yes, plenty of time to go into all that on my plane.
Mrs Pullen Very well, if you say so, Abdul.

Marami Hasn't she got a musical voice? It tinkles like a mountain stream. I hope it goes on for ever and ever.
Pullen (*with feeling*) Oh, it does.
Rubinstein All we need now is my signature and yours, Mrs Pullen, and don't forget to add your address and occupation.
Mrs Pullen (*signing*) Oh yes. What's our address, Abdul?
Marami Care of Sheik Marami, Marami Palace, Marami.
Mrs Pullen Oh yes, sounds so romantic.
Rubinstein And your occupation.

Mrs Pullen writes it in

Mrs Pullen Is that the right spelling for concubine?
Pullen That'll look good on your passport.
Mrs Pullen Oh yes, I shall need one of those, Abdul.
Marami I will add you to mine.
Pullen With all the others, no doubt.
Rubinstein (*signing hurriedly*) Well, it's been a pleasure doing business with you, gentlemen. (*He collects his case and hat, and goes to the main doors*) If I hurry I'll just be in time for Schule. I've got a hire car outside.
Marami Driven by your cousin, no doubt.
Rubinstein (*laughing*) No, no. Believe it or not, car hire is the one business I don't have any cousins in. This is my Rabbi's cousin.

Rubinstein exits, leaving the door open

Marami Are you ready to leave now, Jasmine? (*He rises and goes to the desk with the documents*)
Mrs Pullen Yes, Abdul. It's been quite an exciting morning, hasn't it?
Marami Very stimulating. But the greatest bonus of the day is the acquisition of my Jasmine. (*He extends his hand to her*) Come.

Mrs Pullen goes to Marami

Valerie enters from the kitchen with a champagne bucket, and the champagne already opened

Mrs Pullen I think I must be the luckiest girl in England. (*To Pullen*) And I hope your luck changes too.
Pullen It has!

Marami and Mrs Pullen move to the main doors. Marami slaps Mrs Pullen playfully on the bottom

Mrs Pullen (*with a squeal of delight*) Oh, cheeky sheiky.

Marami and Mrs Pullen exit by main door, leaving it open

Valerie goes to the drinks cabinet, gets a napkin and wraps it round the champagne bottle

Sir Frederick You've given an admirable performance, Pullen. No-one would ever know how heartbroken you are.
Pullen My performance must be better than I thought.

Act II

Sir Frederick (*surprised*) What do you mean?
Pullen Can you imagine what it's like being cooped up with that woman for twenty-five years? Twenty-five years of being waved off to the eight oh-nine from Coulsdon South clutching those soggy sandwiches?
Sir Frederick At least you had a nice break every year in Bournemouth.
Pullen Bugger Bournemouth.
Valerie Wait a minute. I thought you were divorced from her and married to Stella now.

Pullen goes to Valerie

Pullen That, my dear Valerie, was a little fib invented to spare your feelings and your husband's skin.
Valerie You mean she was one of his tarts?
Pullen In a word, yes.
Valerie He's made his bed for good now, and he can lie in it.
Pullen As long as I can lie in yours.
Valerie Let's get the champers going and launch our new life.
Sir Frederick Don't let it go to your head, Pullen.
Pullen The name's Holbrook, and don't you forget it.
Sir Frederick It's been a remarkable turn of events, you ought to be in the *Guinness Book of Records*.
Pullen What for?
Sir Frederick The quickest fortune ever made—and the sharpest.
Valerie Will you join us in a glass, Freddie?
Pullen No!

Sir Frederick rises, goes to the main doors and collects his hat, stick and case

Sir Frederick No, if you don't mind I must get back to Downing Street, and then make arrangements for your husband, Valerie, to be transported to Australia as soon as the doctor thinks he's well enough.
Valerie Yes, he'll want to keep pace with all the other rams, won't he?
Sir Frederick He may not have been a perfect husband, but he made up for it in other ways.
Valerie Sure, by being a perfect rotter.
Sir Frederick Well, Pullen, I can only say ...
Pullen Holbrook!
Sir Frederick (*apologetically*) I'm sorry—Holbrook. I suppose we should be grateful to you.
Pullen You certainly should.
Sir Frederick A word of advice: don't abuse your position. Always remember you're one of us now, a gentleman. Good-day.

Sir Frederick exits through the main doors

Valerie goes to Pullen and gives him a glass of champagne, keeping one herself

Valerie To us!
Pullen To you, my darling, and to our new life in South America?
Valerie South America?

Pullen Of course, we leave tonight.
Valerie It's going to be intriguing, finding out about each other.
Pullen Very.
Valerie For instance, which end of the bath do you sit?
Pullen (*almost unable to believe his good fortune*) The one facing you.
Valerie Do you think we have time for one now?
Pullen (*impishly*) Run one and see.

Valerie exits to bedroom

Pullen goes to the bedroom door and then to the balcony to survey the scene of the City. The faint sound of church bells is heard. He returns and sits at the desk chair, and takes off his glasses, picks up a cigar and cigar-cutter and cuts the cigar. He lights the cigar and coughs very slightly. The bells fade down. He puts two feet on the desk. The telephone rings. He lifts the receiver

(*On the phone*) Hello, Sir Justin Holbrook here... Ah, Mount Street Secretarial Agency... No, Miss Richards has just left...

Valerie enters from the bedroom in a short towelling bathrobe

And by the way, I want to cancel the Holbrook account...

Valerie exits to the bedroom

For the time being!

Pullen puts the receiver down, sits back, and takes a puff of his cigar, as—

the CURTAIN *falls*

FURNITURE AND PROPERTY LIST

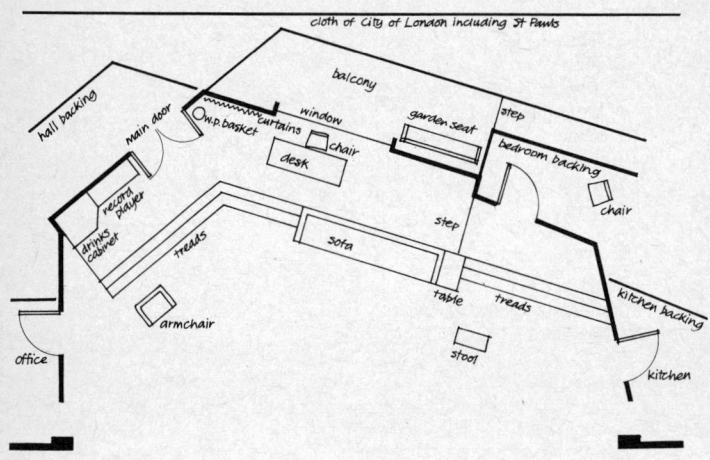

ACT I

On stage: Sofa
Stool
Armchair
Bench on balcony
Desk chair
Desk. *On it:* blotter, letters, letter-head, diary, notepad, address book, ashtray, pencils in pot, **Holbrook's** glasses, pen stand, 2 pens, cigar-cutter, lighter, box of cigars, pocket calculator, telephone (off the hook). *In top drawer:* bottle of tablets, bunch of keys. *On floor above:* trick telephone. *Beside it:* waste-paper basket
Drinks cabinet. *On it:* soda syphon, ice bucket, bottle of whisky, whisky tumbler, jug of water, 2 napkins, lamp. *On shelves above:* brandy glasses, whisky tumblers, champagne glasses
Sofa table. *On it:* dirty brandy glass, cigarette-box, lighter, ashtray
Record-player with record playing
On floor: **Stella's** shoes
Plant in stand
Key in office door
Carpet
Window curtains

Off stage: 2 glasses of orange juice (**Holbrook**)
Glass of water (**Stella**)
Overnight bag (**Stella**)
Blanket (**Holbrook**)
Briefcase (**Pullen**)
Umbrella (**Pullen**)
Briefcase, hat, walking-stick (**Goudhurst**)
Suitcase, handbag, gloves (**Mrs Pullen**)
Handbag, shawl (**Lady Valerie**)

Personal: **Pullen**: glasses, hat, macintosh
Stella: watch
Holbrook: watch, handkerchief
Marami: watch, pen
Goudhurst: watch, handkerchief
Rubinstein: watch, pen
Cornish: watch

ACT II

Strike: Dirty glasses
Holbrook's handkerchief
Mrs Pullen's suitcase

Off stage: Knife (**Marami**)
Tray with teapot, milk jug, sugar bowl, cup, saucer, teaspoon (**Goudhurst**)
Champagne bottle in bucket (**Valerie**)
British Airways bag (**Holbrook**)
Torn documents (**Rubinstein**)
Suitcase (**Holbrook**)
Briefcase, hat (**Rubinstein**)
Doctor's bag (**Cornish**)
Bottle of tablets (**Marami**)
2 lots of papers (**Rubinstein**)
Sellotaped papers (**Rubinstein**)

LIGHTING PLOT

Property fittings required: wall lights, lamp (dressing only)
An apartment. The same scene throughout

ACT I   Morning
To open: General effect of early morning sunshine
No cues

ACT II   Morning
To open: As Act I
No cues

EFFECTS PLOT

ACT I

Cue 1	**As Curtain** rises *Music from record-player*	(Page 1)
Cue 2	**Holbrook** stops record *Music off*	(Page 1)
Cue 3	**Pullen** goes to bedroom *Telephone rings*	(Page 17)
Cue 4	**Marami:** "... he works on a Saturday" *Telephone rings*	(Page 20)

ACT II

Cue 5	**Mrs Pullen:** "... I want a doctor" *Telephone rings*	(Page 29)
Cue 6	**Pullen:** "... can be on our way" *Telephone rings*	(Page 41)
Cue 7	**Pullen:** "... end of the bath do you sit?" *Faint sound of street traffic*	(Page 56)
Cue 8	**Pullen** goes to balcony *Distant church bells: fade, with traffic sounds, as telephone rings*	(Page 56)
Cue 9	**Pullen** puts feet on desk *Telephone rings*	(Page 56)

Printed in Great Britain by Butler & Tanner Ltd, Frome and London